USING COMPUTERIZE

USING COMPUTERIZED SPREADSHEETS

MATHEMATICS FOR RETAIL BUYING

Linda M. Cushman

SYRACUSE UNIVERSITY

FAIRCHILD PUBLICATIONS, INC.

New York, NY

Executive Editor: Olga T. Kontzias
Acquisitions Editor: Joseph Miranda
Assistant Acquisitions Editor: Jason Moring
Art Director: Adam B. Bohannon
Director of Production: Priscilla Taguer
Associate Production Editor: Beth Applebome
Assistant Editor: Suzette Lam
Publishing Assistant: Jaclyn Bergeron
Copy Editor: Words and Numbers
Interior Design: Andrew Katz
Cover Design: Adam B. Bohannon

Library of Congress Catalog Card Number: 2004101071
ISBN: 1-56367-336-3

GST R 133004424
Printed in the United States of America

CONTENTS

EXTENDED CONTENTS

PREFACE

FORMAT OF THE WORKBOOK

This workbook is designed to help you develop computerized spreadsheet skills and recognize the usefulness of applying those skills to the mathematical calculations necessary for retail buying. The workbook is a supplemental text for textbooks in retail mathematics and retail buying. The lessons and practice problems are meant to help you apply concepts learned in your retail math text and/or from your instructor to spreadsheet operations. Although this book is written as a supplement to *Mathematics for Retail Buying* by Bette Tepper, the concepts are easily adaptable to any text meant to cover the mathematical concepts associated with retail buying.

Many students are at least somewhat familiar with Microsoft Excel. This workbook is designed for those with very little computer/spreadsheet knowledge. Each lesson provides step-by-step instructions for performing a variety of computerized spreadsheet tasks and applying a broad range of retail math concepts in those spreadsheet operations. Each workbook includes a CD-ROM that contains a set of preprogrammed worksheets to be used with each of the lessons and some of the practice problems. You will be instructed at the beginning of each exercise which file will need to be opened. Although you will not be able to save files to the CD provided, instructions will also be given for saving your work on the hard drive of your computer or on a separate disk.

In addition to the step-by-step lesson, practice problems are provided to allow you the freedom to format your own spreadsheet to provide a solution to the given scenario. You can refer to the step-by-step lesson for professional presentation and formatting tips.

Computerized spreadsheets are only as accurate as the information and formulas that are entered. However, the presentation of material in spreadsheet format can be a useful tool in communicating information and performance results. Buyers and merchandisers manipulate data every day with the assistance of computerized spreadsheets to reduce the time spent making mathematical calculations and organizing data. The lessons and practice problems you complete in this workbook will provide you with a portfolio that represents your skills and abilities with respect to retail buying concepts, spreadsheet operations, and professional presentation of materials.

ACKNOWLEDGMENTS

The author is most grateful to the reviewers selected by the publisher who offered their expertise and suggestions for improvement. Reviewers included Ann Fairhurst, University of Tennessee—Knoxville; Karen Guthrie, Virginia Commonwealth University; Nancy Miller, University of Nebraska—Lincoln; and Leslie Stoel, Ohio State University.

Finally, the author would like to thank the editors, designers, and production team at Fairchild for their patience, guidance, and encouragement in completing this project.

INTRODUCTION TO USING COMPUTERIZED SPREADSHEETS

Throughout this workbook, you will use computerized spreadsheets to perform the mathematical calculations associated with merchandising. In this first chapter, you will have a chance to practice many of the basic spreadsheet operations as well as the types of formula writing that will be used in subsequent chapters. As you work your way through the rest of the chapters, you will be reminded to refer to the instructions in this chapter if you have forgotten how to perform the operations required in the lesson.

LESSON 1 BASIC SPREADSHEET OPERATIONS

Opening a File

1. Open Excel. It is usually located on your desktop as an icon. It can also be accessed from the **Start** menu in the bottom left-hand corner of your screen.

	A	B	C	D	E	F	G	H
1								
2								
3								
4			Sales		Sales			
5			Year 1		Year 2		% Change	
6	Quarter 1							
7	Quarter 2							
8	Quarter 3							
9	Quarter 4							
10	Yearly Total							
11								
12								
13								
14								
15								
16								
17								
18								
19								
20								
21								
22								
23								
24								
25								

FIGURE 1.1

2. Place the CD, which you will find enclosed with this book, into your computer. From the **File** menu, click **Open** and then locate the file **Lesson1.xls**. You can open this file by double clicking on the file name.

3. Your screen should resemble Figure 1.1.

4. Use file **Lesson1.xls** to perform the following tasks:

Entering Data

5. To enter data in a cell, click on the cell and type. When you have typed the

information, press **Enter** or click on the green check mark (✔) in the formula bar. Now, enter the following data in the appropriate cells:

Sales Year 1 − Quarter 1 = 40,000	Sales Year 2 − Quarter 1 = 43,000
Sales Year 1 − Quarter 2 = 38,000	Sales Year 2 − Quarter 2 = 41,000
Sales Year 1 − Quarter 3 = 41,000	Sales Year 2 − Quarter 3 = 44,000
Sales Year 1 − Quarter 4 = 48,000	Sales Year 2 − Quarter 4 = 53,000

Formatting the Numbers

6. The sales figures you have just entered need to be represented as dollar amounts. Each cell in the Excel spreadsheet is formatted as **General** by default. These cells, which represent dollar sales figures, need to be formatted as currency.
7. Place your cursor in cell **C6**. Click on the cell. Hold the left mouse button down, drag your cursor down to cell **C10**, and then release the button. The highlighted area can now be formatted. Click on **Format** and select **Cells**. Select the **Number** tab from the box that appears and then click on **Currency**. In the Sample box, you can see how your formatting will look. Press **Enter** to indicate that the selection is correct.
8. Repeat this process in cells **E6** through **E10**.

Formula Writing

9. Working in cell **C10**, click on the **Autosum (Σ)** symbol located in the formatting bar. You will notice that a flashing box forms around the data you entered in cells **C6** through **C9** and a suggested formula appears in the active cell, **C10**. This formula =**SUM(C6:C9)** suggests that you want to add the data in the cells that are encircled by the flashing box. The formula should be correct, so you can press **Enter** or click on the check mark (✔).

10. If the formula is incorrect, press the **Backspace** key one time. Now your cursor is flashing within the parentheses in the selected cell. Without moving the cursor, type the following: **C6:C9** (type with no spaces). Press the **Enter** key or click on the check mark (✔). A yearly total should appear in cell **C10**. Your screen should resemble Figure 1.2.

☼ HINT   You should always estimate the sum and double-check that the formula you have created gives you a reasonable answer.

FIGURE 1.2

	A	B	C	D	E	F	G	H
1								
2								
3								
4			Sales		Sales			
5			Year 1		Year 2		% Change	
6	Quarter 1		40,000		43,000			
7	Quarter 2		38,000		41,000			
8	Quarter 3		41,000		44,000			
9	Quarter 4		48,000		53,000			
10	Yearly Total		167,000					
11								
12								
13								
14								
15								
16								
17								
18								
19								
20								
21								
22								
23								
24								
25								
26								

Figure1.2.xls

Sheet1 / Sheet2 / Sheet3 /

Ready   CAPS NUM

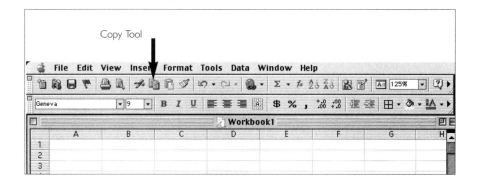

FIGURE 1.3

Copying a Formula

11. Click on cell **C10**, and then click on the **Copy** tool in the toolbar. Or, click on **Edit** and choose **Copy** from the pull-down menu. You should see a flashing box form around cell **C10**. Next, click on cell **E10** and press the **Paste** tool located in the toolbar. Or, click on **Edit** and choose **Paste** from the pull-down menu. A yearly total should appear in cell **E10**. Refer to Figure 1.3 to see where to find the **Copy** tool.

☀ HINT   Using the copy and paste functions allows the formula to change to include the identical set of cells, but from a different column. Check the formula bar: Where your original formula reads =**SUM(C6:C9)**, the newly pasted formula now reads =**SUM(E6:E9)**.

Creating a Formula

12. To determine the percent change in sales for the two-year period, calculate

$$\frac{\text{TY Sales} - \text{LY Sales}}{\text{LY Sales}}$$

TY = This Year, LY = Last Year

(in this example TY = Year 2 and LY = Year 1)

13. On your spreadsheet with your cursor active in cell **G6**, type the following formula: **=(E6-C6)/C6** (with no spaces).

14. When you are finished typing the formula, press **Enter** or click on the check mark (✔).

☼ HINT   Don't panic when you see a number with a decimal in the cell where the formula was created. The cell is not formatted for percentages yet. The next few steps will describe how to format the cell for percentages.

Completing the Formatting

15. Use the copy and paste functions as you did in Step 11 to find the percent change for the remaining three quarters and for the year.

☼ HINT   When you are ready to select the cell you wish to copy the formula into, you can click on the first cell (**G7** in this case). Then hold down the left mouse button to highlight each cell in which you would like the formula to be copied (**G7** through **G10**). When the proper cells are highlighted, the first cell, **G7**, will appear white but the following cells will be darkened. Release the left mouse button and continue by selecting the paste function.

Formatting a Cell

16. Now that you have completed the percent change in sales for the two year periods, you will want to format these decimal answers into percent format. Click on cell **G6** and hold down the left mouse button while dragging down to **G10**.

17. When the cells are highlighted, click on **Format** in the menu bar then select **Cells**. A window will open with several tabbed pages. The open page is the Number Formatting page and in the list of selections on the left you should see the choice **Percentage**.

18. Select **Percentage** and then check to make sure that the number of decimal places specified (on the right-hand side of the box) indicates that **2** decimal places will be displayed. Then select **OK** at the bottom of the open window to complete the formatting function.

☀ HINT   The number of decimal places can be changed as necessary by either clicking on the up arrow or by typing in the desired number of decimal places. However, if you include too many digits after the decimal, the spreadsheet can become confusing to read. Your instructor may have a preference about the number of decimal places to be used when formatting currency and percentages; otherwise, use what is indicated by the text.

Centering Data in a Cell

19. Your calculations are complete for this assignment. Before you learn to save your work and print out a copy for grading, you need to format the spreadsheet in a way that is visually pleasing, easy to read, and professional.

20. Click on cell **C4** and hold down the left mouse button while dragging down to cell **C10** and over to (and including the figures in) column **G10**.

21. When this area is highlighted, you can select **Format** and **Cells** just as you did in Step 17.

22. When the cell-formatting window opens, select the tabbed page that contains the heading **Alignment**. You will see a small pull-down menu labeled **Horizontal**. Click on the downward pointing arrow to the right of the menu. A list of options will appear. Click on **Center**. Then choose **OK**.

☼ HINT   After highlighting the cells you wish to center, you can also simply click the **Center** button in the formula bar. There are four buttons showing various line sets—left alignment, center alignment, right alignment, and full justification.

Creating Bold Headings

23. Hold down the left mouse button and drag to select the row titles Quarter 1 through Yearly Total (**A6** through **A10**). Release the left mouse button and press the **B** in the formatting toolbar.

24. Repeat this process, highlighting cells **C4** and **C5** through **G4** and **G5** to make the column headings in the table bold.

☼ HINT   This is a good time to make sure that the font is consistent throughout the table. Highlight the entire table by clicking on cell **A4** and dragging to **G10**. Then select **Format**, **Cells**, and **Font** and you may select the font and point size that you desire. Finally, click **OK**.

Placing a Border Under Column Headings

25. Hold down the left mouse button and highlight cells **C5** through **G5**. Then select **Format** from the menu bar and select **Cells**.

26. When the formatting window opens, select the tab labeled **Border**. You will see to the right of the window a variety of line selections. Choose the type of line you prefer.

27. Under the **Border** section of the window, you can select from a variety of buttons to indicate where you want to place a border in the cell. Choose the button that places a border only on the bottom of the selected cells.

28. When you have completed these steps, click **OK** to close the window. The border you have chosen is underneath the column headings on your spreadsheet.

29. Although your formatting choices may differ slightly, your screen should resemble Figure 1.4. Your answers will appear as they do in the figure if you have written your formulas correctly.

✳ HINT   If you are unhappy with your border selection, leave the cells highlighted and go through the steps again, but choose a different line before selecting the bottom border. Remember, the goal is for your spreadsheet to look professional.

Setting a Print Area and Formatting the Page

30. Now you are almost ready to complete the assignment. First, set the area of the spreadsheet that you would like to print. Click on cell **A1** and highlight down to cell **I10**. Then select **File** from the menu bar and click on **Print Area/Set Print Area**.

	A	B	C	D	E	F	G	H
1								
2								
3								
4			**Sales**		**Sales**			
5			**Year 1**		**Year 2**		**% Change**	
6	Quarter 1		40,000		43,000		7.50%	
7	Quarter 2		38,000		41,000		7.89%	
8	Quarter 3		41,000		44,000		7.32%	
9	Quarter 4		48,000		53,000		10.42%	
10	Yearly Total		167,000		181,000		8.38%	
11								
12								
13								
14								
15								
16								
17								
18								
19								
20								
21								
22								
23								
24								
25								

Sheet1 / Sheet2 / Sheet3 /
Ready   CAPS NUM

FIGURE 1.4

31. Next, select **File** again and this time click on the **Page Setup** option. When the tabbed window opens, select the tab labeled **Sheet**. You will see that the gridlines and row/column headings have a check mark (✔) beside them. Click on these to eliminate the (✔) and turn off the gridlines and row/column headings.

32. You can select **Print Preview** to see how your spreadsheet will look when printed.

33. When you are through previewing the page, choose **Close** to take you back to your working spreadsheet.

Saving Your Work and Printing

34. Before you print and turn in your assignment, save your work. You should save often during your work session to be sure that you have saved changes made to the worksheet.

35. To save your work, select **File** from the menu bar and then click on **Save As**. You will want to save your work on the A drive (your diskette) and label it **Lesson1**(your initials here with no spaces). For example, if your name is Amy Scott, your file name will read **Lesson1AS**. By labeling the exercise in this way, you can retain the *original* spreadsheet file just in case you should need it at a later date.

36. To save the file on your diskette, place your diskette in the computer diskette slot and then follow the directions above. When the **Save As** window is open you will see a category called **Save In:** and a pull-down menu. Click the down arrow and a variety of choices will appear in the pull-down menu. Select **3 1/2 Floppy (A):** or other appropriate drive as indicated by your instructor. In the category labeled File Name, type the title—**Lesson1**(your initials here with no spaces).

37. After defining the appropriate drive and file name, click **Save**, which is located at the bottom of the open window. Now, print out your assignment by selecting **File**, then **Print** (make the appropriate printer choices for your computer) and press **OK**.

☼ HINT — You may want to save each assignment on more than one diskette or on the hard drive in your own designated folder if you are allowed to do so.

Printing Formulas

38. Your instructor may request that you also print out your spreadsheet assignment showing all the formulas you have written.
39. To do this, select **Tools** and then **Options** from the pull-down menu. Click on the **View** tab and place a check mark (✔) in the **Formulas** box.
40. You can also display formulas by pressing **Ctrl** and the **tilde key** (~).

ADDITIONAL SPREADSHEET OPERATIONS

The skills covered so far are some of the most common and useful for representing retail mathematical operations in spreadsheet form. Here are a few more skills that you might find helpful to employ.

Wrapping Text

1. When you type in text that is too large to fit in one cell, the text will spill over into the next cell. If, however, that cell contains data, the text in your active cell cannot be seen.
2. You can wrap the text to add another line to the desired cell. Place your cursor in the cell, and click on **Format** and then **Cells**. When the window opens, select the **Alignment** tab and then place a check mark (✔) in the box indicating **Wrap text**.

Widening Column Width

1. Sometimes when you insert a formula in a cell the result will be "######."

This usually happens when the cell is not formatted yet (e.g., formatted as a percentage with two decimal places).

2. If the cell is formatted properly, then you need to widen the column by using the **Format** menu and then selecting **Column** and then **Width**. Widen only as much as necessary to reveal the results and remove the "######" symbol. You can also widen the column by placing your cursor on the dividing line to the right side of the column you wish to widen in the column headings (e.g., the line between A and B). When placed above the line, your cursor will become a two-way arrow pointing left and right with a thick center line. Hold down the left mouse button and drag the column to the width of your choice.

PRACTICE PROBLEM

Practice Problem 1.1

Bob Thomas, the manager for men's shirts at Crisalli's Department Store, is very excited about the department's increases in sales in the third and fourth quarters. You mention to Bob that although sales are up overall, you are concerned about the performance of one particular vendor, Alta Vista. You have merchandised the area that Alta Vista occupies and you do not think the merchandise is moving as well as it should. Bob says he knows you have good instincts but he needs facts to support them. He asks you to put together an analysis of sales increases for men's shirts by vendor. While thinking to yourself, "Don't they have a computer program that does this on a daily basis . . . if not on an hourly basis!?", you agree to take on the task.

After digging through stacks and stacks of paperwork, you uncover the following quarterly sales figures:

	Q1	Q2	Q3	Q4
Scott Shirts	$1,550	$1,375	$1,640	$1,890
Max 'n Company	750	890	1,020	1,270
Burbar	395	350	680	875
Lucky Look	2,010	2,440	3,980	4,800
Alta Vista	780	890	1,005	980

Open a blank Excel spreadsheet. Save the blank spreadsheet and give it an appropriate file name. To be consistent, this file should be named **Practice1.1**(your initials here with no spaces). Now you are ready to begin working. Give your table an appropriate title and make sure it is formatted professionally.

Read the situation carefully and use the information that will help you make your point clear to Bob. You can refer to Lesson 1 for some pointers on formatting, calculations, and other spreadsheet operations.

☼ HINT   Your manager is interested in the performance increases from the third to fourth quarter. You can prove your point by highlighting the change in vendor data for Q3 and Q4.

When your assignment is complete, save your work and print out the final results.

2 PROFIT AND LOSS STATEMENTS

The profit and loss statement (P&L) is a summary of the income and expenditures of a business. Frequently called an income statement, this document generally contains a wealth of information. For this lesson, you will be using only the most basic concepts in a skeletal P&L statement to help you examine the relationship between income and expenses. A skeletal P&L is calculated as follows:

Net sales
− Cost of merchandise sold

Gross margin
− Operating expenses

Profit (Loss)

DEFINITIONS

net sales: The total sales for any given period after deducting customer returns and allowances from gross sales.

billed cost: Purchase price as it appears on the invoice.

cost of merchandise sold: Billed cost of the merchandise purchased, plus freight or transportation costs, plus alteration/workroom costs, minus any cash discounts earned.

gross margin: Sometimes referred to as gross profit, this figure is obtained by subtracting the cost of goods sold from net sales.

operating expense: The expenses incurred by the retailer during any given period; usually divided into direct and indirect expenses.

direct expenses: Expenses that exist in a given department that are directly related to that department's business. These expenses would cease to exist if the department ceased to exist.

indirect expenses: Expenses that are incurred that are not directly related to any given department. Examples might include store maintenance and security. Such expenses are usually distributed among the individual departments on the basis of sales volume.

LESSON 2 BASIC PROFIT AND LOSS CALCULATIONS

Opening the File

1. Open Excel. You can refer to Chapter 1 at any time during this lesson if you cannot remember how to perform the assigned tasks.
2. From the **File** menu, click **Open** and then locate the file **Lesson2.xls.** Open this file by double clicking on the file name. Your screen should resemble Figure 2.1.

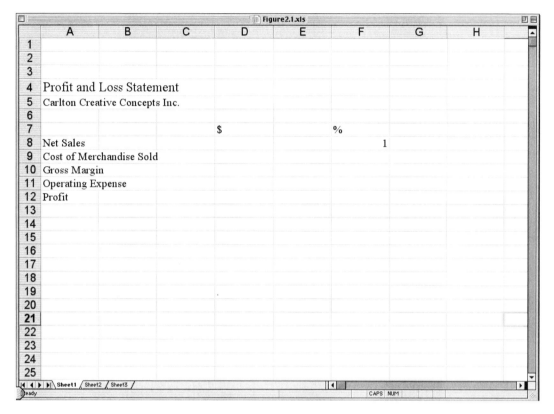

FIGURE 2.1

3. Use file **Lesson2.xls** to perform the following tasks:

Completing the Spreadsheet

4. Enter the following data in Column D in the appropriate cells:

Net sales = 500,000
Cost of merchandise sold = 270,000
Operating expenses = 240,000

☼ HINT   The dollar amounts will be formatted in a later step. For now, enter the figures as shown. If any of the variables had been given as a percentage, you would enter the number as a decimal. Note that the spreadsheet already indicates a 1 for net sales. This will later be formatted to indicate 100%.

---

5. Write the formula in cell **D10** to calculate the gross margin for Carlton Creative Concepts Inc.: **=D8-D9.**

☼ HINT   Remember that all formulas start with an (=), and that subtraction is represented by the hyphen (-) key.

---

6. Write the formula (in cell **D12**) to calculate the profit or (loss) for the company: **=D10-D11.**

☼ HINT   Always estimate the sum and double-check that the formula you have created gives you a reasonable answer.

Calculating Percentages

The five major components of the P&L statement can be expressed as a percentage of sales. Percentages allow the business to easily compare performance on a year-to-year basis and a business-to-business basis. For example, $5,000 profit on $500,000 sales is not nearly as impressive as $5,000 profit on $50,000 sales (a 1% profit versus a 10% profit).

7. Calculate the remaining three components, dividing each component by net sales. Your screen should resemble Figure 2.2.

☀ HINT   Remember that net sales will always be equal to 100% and all other components must be expressed as a percentage of net sales. Therefore, the formula for calculating cost of merchandise sold as a percent to net sales should read: **=D9/D8.**

FIGURE 2.2

	A	B	C	D	E	F	G	H
1								
2								
3								
4	Profit and Loss Statement							
5	Carlton Creative Concepts Inc.							
6								
7				$		%		
8	Net Sales			500000		1		
9	Cost of Merchandise Sold			270000		0.54		
10	Gross Margin			230000		0.46		
11	Operating Expenses			240000		0.48		
12	Profit			-10000		-0.02		
13								
14								
15								
16								
17								
18								
19								
20								
21								
22								
23								
24								

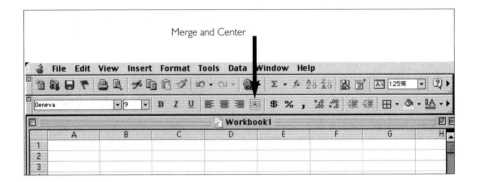

FIGURE 2.3

Formatting the Spreadsheet

To professionally present your spreadsheet calculations, complete the following formatting functions:

8. Center the title for the table. Click on cell **A4** and drag the mouse to **H4**. When the cells are highlighted, click on the **Merge and Center** button located in the formatting bar. This button is located to the right of alignment buttons and appears as an "a" with arrows pointing outward on either side. Refer to Figure 2.3.

9. With cells **A4** through **H4** still highlighted, click the bold **B** in the formatting bar located next to the font size to make the table heading bold.

10. Center the company name in the same manner as described above by highlighting cells **A5** through **H5**.

11. Highlight cells **A8** through **A12** and make the components text bold by clicking on the **B.**

12. Beginning in cell **D7**, hold down the left mouse button and drag down to **D12** and over to **F12**. Now center the text within these columns by clicking the centering alignment key in the formatting bar.

13. Highlight from cell **D8** to **D12**. Then select **Format** and select **Cells** from

the pull-down menu. A window will open with several tabbed pages. The **Number** page is already visible. Select **Currency** from the category menu and make sure that the number of decimal places specified is **0**. You should see another category entitled **Negative numbers**. Select the option that indicates the negative numbers in red and enclosed in parentheses. Click **OK**.

14. Highlight from cell **F8** to **F12**. Then select **Format** and select **Cells** from the pull-down menu. Select **Percentage** from the category menu and make sure that the decimal places are set at **0**. Click **OK**. Your screen should now resemble Figure 2.4.

FIGURE 2.4

	A	B	C	D	E	F	G	H
1								
2								
3								
4				**Profit and Loss Statement**				
5				Carlton Creative Concepts Inc.				
6								
7				$		%		
8	Net Sales			$500,000		100%		
9	Cost of Merchandise Sold			$270,000		54%		
10	Gross Margin			$230,000		46%		
11	Operating Expenses			$240,000		48%		
12	Profit			($10,000)		-2%		
13								
14								
15								
16								
17								
18								
19								
20								
21								
22								
23								
24								
25								

Sheet1 / Sheet2 / Sheet3
CAPS NUM

☼ HINT   Although it is not necessary in this case, sometimes the text you enter will not fit properly in the cell. You can **Wrap** the text in order to add another line to the desired cell. Place your cursor in the cell and click on **Format** and then **Cells**. When the window opens, select the **Alignment** tab and then place a check mark (✔) in the box indicating **Wrap text**. Refer to Figure 2.5.

FIGURE 2.5

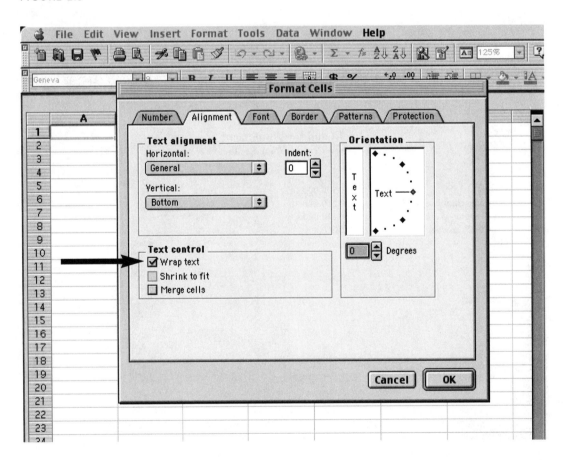

Setting a Print Area and Formatting the Page

15. Now you are almost ready to complete the assignment. Set the area of the spreadsheet that you would like to print. Click on cell **A1** and highlight down to cell **H12**. Then select **File** from the menu bar and click on **Print Area/Set Print Area**.

16. Next, select **File** again and this time click on the **Page Setup** option. When the tabbed window opens, select the tab labeled **Sheet**. You will see that the gridlines and row/column headings have a check mark (✔) beside them. Click on these to eliminate the (✔) and turn off the gridlines and row/column headings.

17. You can select **Print Preview** to see how your spreadsheet will look when printed. When you are through previewing the page, choose **Close** to take you back to your working spreadsheet.

Saving Your Work and Printing

18. Save your work on the drive that contains your diskette and label it **Lesson2.1**(your initials here with no spaces) just as you did in Chapter 1.

19. Now print out your assignment. Save your work to more than one diskette or on the hard drive, if permitted.

Printing Formulas

20. Your instructor may request that you also print out your spreadsheet assignment showing all the formulas you have written. To do this, simply select **Tools** and then **Options** from the pull-down menu. Click on the **View** tab and place a check mark (✔) in the **Formulas** box. [You can also display formulas by pressing **Ctrl** and the **tilde key** (~).]

PRACTICE PROBLEMS

Practice Problem 2.1

Open a blank Excel spreadsheet. Save the blank spreadsheet and give it an appropriate file name. To be consistent, this file should be named **Practice2.1**(your initials here with no spaces). Now you are ready to begin working.

The owners of Carter's Coldwear have just completed what they believe to be a fairly profitable year. Given the following information, create a skeletal P&L statement depicting both dollar amounts and percents for the Carter's company.

Net sales = $242,000
Cost of merchandise sold = $134,600
Operating expenses = 38%

Give your P&L statement an appropriate title and make sure to format it in a professional manner. Be sure to round the dollar values to the nearest dollar and the percents to two decimal places. (You may want to refer to the formatting instructions given in Lesson 1.)

If you do not have access to a color printer to indicate a loss in red, you should make sure that any loss is enclosed in parentheses to indicate that the dollar and percentage figures are losses, not gains.

When your assignment is complete, be sure to save (because you have already saved the file once, click on **File** and then **Save** in the menu bar) your work and print out the final results.

Practice Problem 2.2

Open a blank Excel spreadsheet. Save the blank spreadsheet and name it **Practice2.2**(your initials here with no spaces).

After calculating this year's P&L, the owners of Carter's Coldwear realize that they never completed a P&L for last year. Use the data listed below to create a skeletal P&L statement depicting both dollar amounts and percents.

Net sales = $221,000
Cost of merchandise sold = $119,800
Profit = 16%

When your assignment is complete, save your work and print out the final results as directed by your instructor.

Practice Problem 2.3

Open a blank Excel spreadsheet. Save the blank spreadsheet and name it **Practice2.3**(your initials here with no spaces).

Using the data from Practice Problem 2.1 and Practice Problem 2.2, create a spreadsheet that compares last year's data for Carter's Coldwear (given in Practice Problem 2.2) to this year's data (given in Practice Problem 2.1). Make sure to indicate the percentage change for the components of the profit and loss statements.

If you do not have access to a color printer that allows you to indicate a loss in red, you should enclose the dollar or percentage figure in parentheses.

When your assignment is complete, save your work and print out the final results as directed by your instructor.

Practice Problem 2.4

Open a blank Excel spreadsheet. Save the blank spreadsheet and name it **Practice2.4**(your initials here with no spaces).

The swimwear department at Longmoor's Department Store has the following figures available:

Net sales = $325,000
Cost of goods sold = $213,000
Operating expenses = $88,000

Create a skeletal P&L statement for the swimwear department at Longmoor's depicting both dollars and percentages.

Save your work and print as directed by your instructor.

Practice Problem 2.5

For this assignment, open the spreadsheet you saved in Practice Problem 2.4. Save the blank spreadsheet and name it **Practice2.5**(your initials here with no spaces).

The Divisional Merchandise Manager is planning for a profit of 10% next year. He is convinced that the cost of goods can be controlled to attain this profit level without sacrificing sales or increasing expenses.

Create a second P&L statement that depicts the new cost of goods sold figure necessary to attain a profit level of 10%.

What strategies might the buyer use to reduce the cost of goods? Is it possible to achieve these reductions without sacrificing sales? Write a brief paragraph to explain. You may place your statements at the bottom of the spreadsheet or in a separate Word document as indicated by your instructor.

Save your work and print as directed by your instructor.

Practice Problem 2.6

Open a blank Excel spreadsheet. Save the blank spreadsheet and name it
Practice2.6(your initials here with no spaces).

The shoe buyer for a major Philadelphia department store has attained
a profit of 8% for this year. She was able to maintain a 48% gross margin of
$158,000.

Complete a skeletal P&L for the shoe department that depicts both dollars and percentages for net sales, cost of goods sold, gross margin, operating expenses, and profit.

Save your work and print as directed by your instructor.

3 THE RELATIONSHIP OF MARKUP TO PROFIT

In this chapter, you will be introduced to the basic pricing factors. The retailer must set a price for items offered for resale that covers the cost of the item and an added amount, known as markup (MU). This price must also be large enough to cover the expenses incurred in selling the item and include a desired profit. Markup percentages can be calculated as a percentage of the retail price of the item, or the cost price. Generally, retailers express markup as a percentage of retail, though some retailers still use the cost-based method. Both methods will be presented in this chapter.

FORMULAS

Retail = $Cost + $Markup

$Markup = $Retail − $Cost

$Cost = $Retail − $Markup

$$\text{Cost\%} = \frac{\text{\$Cost}}{\text{\$Retail}}$$

$$\text{Markup\% on retail} = \frac{\text{\$Markup}}{\text{\$Retail}}$$

$$\text{Markup\% on cost} = \frac{\text{\$Markup}}{\text{\$Cost}}$$

$$\text{Retail} = \frac{\text{\$Cost}}{(100\% - \text{Markup\%})}$$

$$\text{Cost} = \text{\$Retail} \times (100\% - \text{Markup\%})$$

$$\text{Markup\% on entire purchase} = \frac{(\text{Total \$retail} - \text{Total \$cost})}{\text{Total \$retail}}$$

LESSON 3 CALCULATING COST, MARKUP, AND RETAIL

Opening the File

1. Open Excel. From the **File** menu, click **Open** and then locate the file **Lesson3.xls.** Open this file by double clicking on the file name. Your screen should resemble Figure 3.1. Letters a–s in the first column will be referred to as problem (a), problem (b), and so on.
2. Using file **Lesson3.xls,** perform the following tasks:

Completing the Spreadsheet

3. Enter the formula in cell **D6** to calculate the $markup for the retail and cost figures given in **B6** and **C6**, respectively: This can be done by clicking

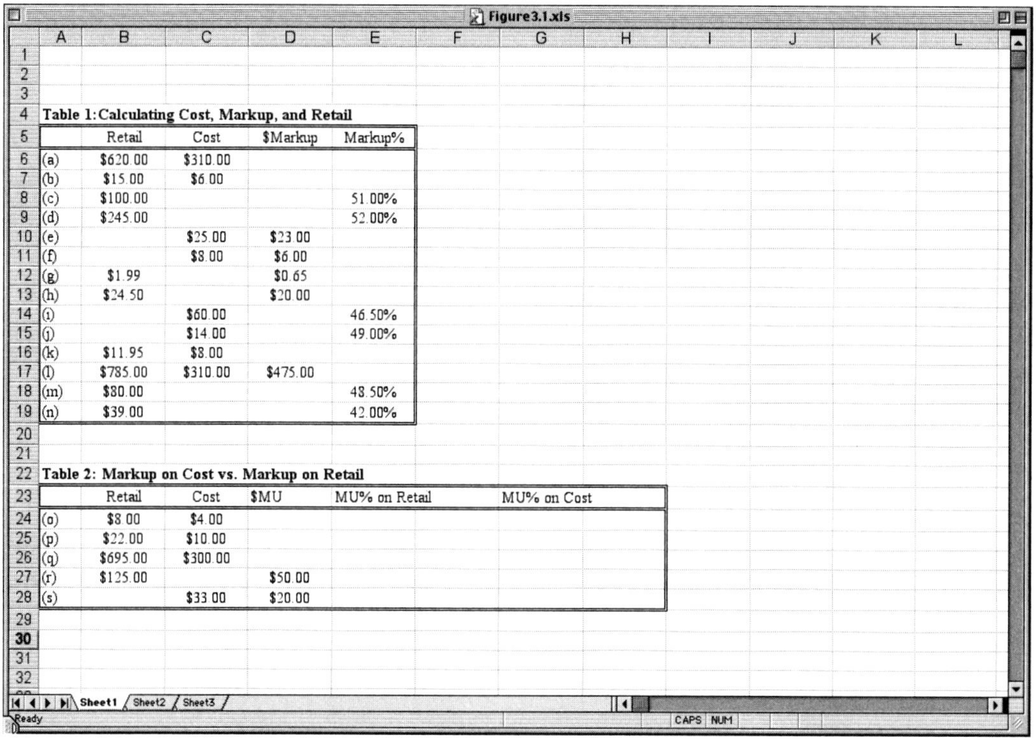

FIGURE 3.1

on cell **D6** and typing: =**B6-C6**. When you have finished typing the formula, press **Enter** or click on the green check mark (✔) in the formula bar.

✻ HINT   Remember that **$Markup = $Retail − $Cost**

---

     4. Write the formula in cell **E6** to calculate the markup% based on retail in problem (a). This can be done by clicking on cell **E6** and typing: =**D6/B6**.

When you have finished typing the formula, press **Enter** or click on the green check mark (✔) in the formula bar.

☼ HINT

The formula for calculating markup at retail can be written (**$Retail** − **$Cost**) ÷ **$Retail**. But it also can be said that **$Markup** = **$Retail** − **$Cost** and **Markup%** = **$Markup** ÷ **$Retail**.

---

5. Copy the formula for $markup that you entered in **D6** into cell **D7**.
6. Repeat the process in Step 5 so that you can copy the formula for markup% that you entered in cell **E6** into cell **E7**.
7. Write the formula to calculate the $cost necessary to complete problem (c). This can be accomplished by typing =**PRODUCT(B8,1-E8)** in cell **C8**. Then you can complete the problem by typing the formula =**B8-C8** in cell **D8**.

☼ HINT

The formula for calculating $cost when $retail and markup% are known is:

$$\text{\$Retail} \times (100\% - \text{Markup\%}) = \text{\$Cost}$$

Although your spreadsheet is formatted to show markup% in percent format, the computer thinks of this figure in decimal form. Therefore, when you write the formula to subtract markup% from 100%, you must use a 1 instead of a 100. As you will remember from Lesson 1, 100% is equivalent to 1.00 in decimal format.

---

8. Use the steps above to copy the formulas written in cells **C8** and **D8** into cells **C9** and **D9**, respectively, in order to complete problem (d).
9. Write the formula in cell **B10** to calculate the $retail necessary to complete problem (e). This can be accomplished by typing =**SUM(C10,D10)**.

Figure 3.2.xls

Table 1: Calculating Cost, Markup, and Retail

	Retail	Cost	$Markup	Markup%
(a)	$620.00	$310.00	$310.00	50.00%
(b)	$15.00	$6.00	$9.00	60.00%
(c)	$100.00	$49.00	$51.00	51.00%
(d)	$245.00	$117.60	$127.40	52.00%
(e)	$48.00	$25.00	$23.00	47.92%
(f)	$14.00	$8.00	$6.00	42.86%
(g)	$1.99		$0.65	
(h)	$24.50		$20.00	
(i)		$60.00		46.50%
(j)		$14.00		49.00%
(k)	$11.95	$8.00		
(l)	$785.00	$310.00	$475.00	
(m)	$80.00			48.50%
(n)	$39.00			42.00%

Table 2: Markup on Cost vs. Markup on Retail

	Retail	Cost	$MU	MU% on Retail	MU% on Cost
(o)	$8.00	$4.00			
(p)	$22.00	$10.00			
(q)	$695.00	$300.00			
(r)	$125.00		$50.00		
(s)		$33.00	$20.00		

FIGURE 3.2

Then you can complete problem (e) by clicking on cell **E10** and typing the formula to calculate Markup%: =**D10/B10**.

10. Use the steps above to copy the formulas written in cells **B10** and **E10** into cells **B11** and **E11**, respectively, in order to complete problem (f). Your screen should resemble Figure 3.2.

11. Copy the formula you entered in cell **E11** into cells **E12** and **E13**. This calculates the markup% given $markup and $retail.

12. Write the formula to calculate the $cost for problems (g) and (h). This can be done by placing your cursor in cell **C12** and typing a formula that

subtracts the $markup from the $retail. Your formula should be written: =B12-D12. Then, copy this formula into cell C13.

13. Write the formula in cell **B14** to calculate $retail given $cost and markup%. Because we are working with individual items in this example, include in your formula a function that calculates the cost of an individual unit, because cost is given per dozen. Your formula should read =C14/(1-E14). You can then copy this formula into cell **B15** to complete problem (j).

☼ HINT   When trying to calculate $retail given $cost and a desired markup%, the formula is:

$$\text{Retail} = \frac{\$\text{Cost}}{(100\% - \text{Markup\%})}$$

Although your spreadsheet is formatted to show markup% in percent format, the computer thinks of this figure in decimal form. Therefore, when you write the formula to subtract markup% from 100%, you must use a **1** instead of a **100.**

---

14. Write the formula in cell **D14** to calculate $markup. This can be done by subtracting $cost from $retail. The formula reads =B14-C14. After you have typed the formula, press **Enter** or click on the green check mark (✔). This formula can be copied into cells **D15** and **D16** to calculate $markup for problems (j) and (k).

15. Write the formula in cell **E16** to calculate markup% given $markup and $retail. As in Step 2, the formula will read **$Markup ÷ $Retail** or =D16/B16. This formula can then be copied into cell **E17** to complete problem (l).

16. Write the formula in cell **C18** to calculate $cost given $retail and markup%. Your formula will read =PRODUCT(B18, 1-E18). Copy this formula into cell **C19** to calculate $cost for problem (n).

☼ HINT   After copying the formula you will notice that the border in **cell 19** disappears. Reformat the cell as explained in Lesson 1.

17. Write the formula in cell **D18** to subtract $cost from $retail to give you $markup. Your formula will read =**B18-C18**. Copy this formula into cell **D19** to complete the exercise.

Completing the Table

Use the following steps to complete the table: (By now, the formulas should be familiar to you but you can refer to the steps above for help if necessary.)

18. Calculate $markup for problems (o), (p), and (q).
19. Calculate the $cost for problem (r).
20. Calculate the $retail for problem (s).
21. Calculate the markup% based on retail for problem (o) in cell **E24**. The formula will read:

$$\text{Markup\%} = \text{\$Markup} \div \text{\$Retail or} = \text{D24/B24}$$

22. Copy this formula into cells **E25** through **E28**.
23. Remember that the retail calculation of markup is generally used because most other retail financial elements are also calculated as a percentage of retail sales.
24. Calculate the markup% based on $cost for problem (o) in cell **G24**. The formula will read:

$$\text{Markup\%} = \text{\$Markup} \div \text{\$Cost or} = \text{D24/C24}$$

25. Copy this formula into cells **G25** through **G28**.
26. Place your cursor in cell **E24**, and hold down the left mouse button and drag over to **H24** and down to **H28**. Release the left mouse button and the

cells will be highlighted (indicated by the dark black color). Format these cells as percents to two decimal places and press **OK**.

27. Before printing the lesson, place your cursor on the letter A in Column A. You will notice that the entire column is now highlighted. Then select **Insert** and **Column** to add a new column. Your work should now reside in Columns B through I.

28. Take one last look at your work. Make sure that your font is consistent in every cell and table. In this case Times New Roman 10 pt. font was used. Your screen should now look like Figure 3.3.

FIGURE 3.3

Table 1: Calculating Cost, Markup, and Retail

	Retail	Cost	$Markup	%Markup
(a)	$620.00	$310.00	$310.00	50.00%
(b)	$15.00	$6.00	$9.00	60.00%
(c)	$100.00	$49.00	$51.00	51.00%
(d)	$245.00	$117.60	$127.40	52.00%
(e)	$48.00	$25.00	$23.00	47.92%
(f)	$14.00	$8.00	$6.00	42.86%
(g)	$1.99	$1.34	$0.65	32.66%
(h)	$24.50	$4.50	$20.00	81.63%
(i)	$112.15	$60.00	$52.15	46.50%
(j)	$27.45	$14.00	$13.45	49.00%
(k)	$11.95	$8.00	$3.95	33.05%
(l)	$785.00	$310.00	$475.00	60.51%
(m)	$80.00	$41.20	$38.80	48.50%
(n)	$39.00	$22.62	$16.38	42.00%

Table 2: Markup on Cost vs. Markup on Retail

	Retail	Cost	$MU	MU% on Retail	MU% on Cost
(o)	$8.00	$4.00	$4.00	50.00%	100.00%
(p)	$22.00	$10.00	$12.00	54.55%	120.00%
(q)	$695.00	$300.00	$395.00	56.83%	131.67%
(r)	$125.00	$75.00	$50.00	40.00%	66.67%
(s)	$53.00	$33.00	$20.00	37.74%	60.61%

Setting a Print Area and Formatting the Page

29. Set the area of the spreadsheet that you would like to print. Click on cell **A1** and highlight down to cell **I29**. Then select **File** from the menu bar and click on **Print Area/Set Print Area**.

30. Select **File** again, and click on the **Page Setup** option. Select the tab labeled **Sheet**. Select **Print Preview** to see how your spreadsheet will look when printed. When you are through previewing the page, choose **Close** to take you back to your working spreadsheet.

Saving Your Work and Printing

31. Save your work on the A drive (your diskette) and label it **Lesson3.1**(your initials here with no spaces).

Printing Formulas

32. Your instructor may request that you also print out your spreadsheet assignment showing all the formulas you have written. Refer to Lesson 1 if you have forgotten how to complete this task.

PRACTICE PROBLEMS

Practice Problem 3.1

Open a blank Excel spreadsheet. Save it as **Practice3.1**(your initials here with no spaces).

The buyer for Bonnie's Boutique made the purchase listed below. Create a chart that depicts the SKU, quantity, $cost per item, $retail per item, $markup per item, markup%, total cost, and total retail for each SKU. Calculate a total $cost, total $retail, and total markup% for the full order.

SKU#	ITEM DESCRIPTION	QUANTITY	$COST	DESIRED MU%
1160781	Knit Skirt	50	$23.00/skirt	52%
2105476	Leopard Print Handbag	36	$144.00/dozen	49%
3350891	Cotton/Poly Blouse	75	$18.00/blouse	54%
3587049	Knit Shirt	50	$15.00/shirt	52%

☀ HINT

Remember that you are asked to represent the $cost and $retail per item so you will want to use a formula that utilizes the desired markup% and the $cost per item to obtain the retail price you will charge for **each** item.

Be sure to save and print your work.

Practice Problem 3.2

Open a blank Excel spreadsheet. Save it as **Practice3.2**(your initials here with no spaces).

For Valentine's Day, a jewelry buyer wishes to run a special $199.00 promotion on several different ruby and diamond items. The group consists of 114 pieces that cost:

- 45 pieces at $85.00 each
- 25 pieces at $101.00 each
- 44 pieces at $75.00 each

Create a table that depicts the $cost, $retail, and markup% on each item as well as the total $cost, $retail, and markup% for the group.

Be sure to save and print your work.

Practice Problem 3.3

Open a blank Excel spreadsheet. Save it as **Practice3.3**(your initials here with no spaces).

A buyer wants to spend $5,000 at retail on new purchases of facial cleanser for the cosmetics department. The department maintains a 55% markup. The buyer needs a minimum of 300 bottles of cleanser to create an adequate product display. Create a table that depicts the minimum cost and retail per bottle that allows the buyer to maintain the required markup and not exceed the planned total expenditure.

The buyer also wishes to compare the possible assortment with an increase of the markup percent to 58%. Add a row (or column depending on the way you have chosen to format your spreadsheet) to your spreadsheet that depicts the cost and retail per bottle that allows the buyer to achieve the maximum total expenditure ($5,000) with a 58% markup.

Be sure to save and print your work.

Practice Problem 3.4

Open a blank Excel spreadsheet. Save it as **Practice3.4**(your initials here with no spaces.

A buyer for men's shirts purchases from several vendors. Create a table that depicts the $cost, markup%, $retail, and total $retail for each purchase given the following information:

VENDOR	QUANTITY	$COST	MARKUP%	$RETAIL	TOTAL $RETAIL
A	58	$12.00	48%	?	?
B	75	?	52%	$42.00	?
C	45	$15.00	?	$40.00	?
D	60	$18.50	50%	?	?

Save and print your work.

Practice Problem 3.5

Open a blank Excel spreadsheet. Save it as **Practice3.5**(your initials here with no spaces).

A notions buyer wishes to run a special $9.99 promotion on several different items. The group consists of 225 pieces that cost:

- 100 pieces at $3.00 each
- 50 pieces at $5.00 each
- 50 pieces at $5.50 each
- 25 pieces at $6.00 each

Create a table that depicts the $cost, $retail, and markup% on each item as well as the total $cost, $retail, and markup% for the group.

Save and print your work.

Practice Problem 3.6

Open a blank Excel spreadsheet. Save it as **Practice3.6**(your initials here with no spaces).

For the following items, create a chart that compares each item when markup is calculated on retail and when markup is calculated on cost:

$COST	$RETAIL	$MARKUP
$9.00	$19.00	$10.00
$37.00	$75.00	$38.00
$100.00	$150.00	$50.00
$1,050.00	$2,500.00	$1,450.00
$200.00	$450.00	$250.00

Save and print your work.

4 REPRICING OF MERCHANDISE

In this chapter, you will learn to identify several different types of markup as well as the markdowns and repricing that help a retailer develop a successful merchandising strategy. The following exercises will allow you to examine the pricing of merchandise from the first price placed on the merchandise (initial retail) to the price received when the item is eventually sold (final selling price). Read the definitions below carefully and look over the formulas given before beginning the lesson.

DEFINITIONS

initial markup: The difference between the billed cost of merchandise as stated on the invoice and the initial retail price placed on the item.

cumulative markup: The markup percentage achieved on a group of goods over a period of time. Usually all goods available plus any new purchases received for an extended period of time. Does not include markdowns.

maintained markup: The difference between net sales and the cost of merchandise sold. Does not include cash discounts, alterations, etc. Although maintained markup is related to gross margin, the latter is adjusted for cash discounts received and any alteration/workroom expenses encountered.

markdown: A reduction in the original or previous price of an item or a group of items.

markdown cancellation: An increase in the retail price of an item or group of items that offsets all or a portion of a previously taken markdown.

net markdown: The difference between total markdowns and any markdown cancellations that occur.

FORMULAS

$Markdown = Original retail price − New retail price

Net sales = Number of items sold × Price paid for each item

$$Markdown\% = \frac{\$Markdown}{Net\ sales}$$

Markdown cancellation = Retail price − Markdown price (Usually multiplied by the number of items marked back up)

Net markdown = Total markdown − Markdown cancellation

Reductions = Markdowns + Employee discounts + Shortages

$$Initial\ markup\% = \frac{Gross\ margin\% + Alterations\% - Cash\ discounts\% + Reductions\%}{Net\ sales\ (100\%) + Reductions\%}$$

$$Cumulative\ markup\% = \frac{Cumulative\ \$markup}{Cumulative\ retail\ dollars}$$

Maintained markup = Net sales − Gross cost of merchandise sold, where:
Gross cost of merchandise sold = Opening inventory + New purchases +
Inward freight − Closing inventory

Gross margin = Net sales − Total cost of merchandise sold, where:
Total cost of merchandise sold = Gross cost of merchandise sold − Cash
discount + Alteration/workroom costs

LESSON 4 PRICE CHANGES

Opening the File

1. Open Excel. From the **File** menu, click **Open** and locate the file **Lesson4.xls**. Open this file by double clicking on the file name. Your screen should resemble Figure 4.1.
2. Use file **Lesson4.xls** to perform the following tasks:

Completing the Spreadsheet

3. Enter the formula in cell **E10** to calculate the net sales percent for the figure given for workroom costs. Your formula should read: =**D10/D7**. When you have finished typing the formula, press **Enter** or click on the green check mark (✔) in the formula bar.
4. Write the formula in cell **E11** to calculate the net sales percent for the figure given for cash discounts and copy this formula for the other operational results. Your formula will read: =**D11/$D$7**.

	Figure4.1.xls	

	A	B	C	D	E	F	G	H	I	J	K	L	M
1													
2													
3				UPSIDE DOWN SHOP									
4				FALL SEASON									
5	The Upside Down Shop had the following operational results for the fall season:												
6				$	%								
7	Net Sales			$75,000	100.00%								
8	Billed Cost of New Purchases			$36,000									
9	Freight			$610									
10	Workroom Costs			$120									
11	Cash Discounts			$1,080									
12	Markdowns			$9,200									
13	Shortages			$840									
14	Gross Cost of Merchandise Sold												
15	Total Cost of Merchandise Sold												
16						$	%						
17			Maintained Markup										
18			Gross Margin										
19													
20	The store had the following plans for the September 1 shipment:												
21				$Cost	$Retail	MU%							
22	Opening Inventory			$72,000	$150,000	52.00%							
23	Purchases-Baby Gym			$8,900	$17,500								
24	Purchases-Bubble Gum			$6,700	$12,200								
25	Purchases-B.O.B.			$2,900	$6,300		Tot. $Cost						
26	Closing Inventory			$64,580			Tot. $Retail						
27													
28	Reductions%												
29	Initial Markup%												
30	Cumulative Markup%												
31													
32	During the Labor Day Sale, the sales data indicated the following results:												
33													
34	Vendor		Item	#In Stock	# Sold	Sales Price	Original Retail						
35	Baby Gym		Layette	50	38	$20	$25						
36	Bubble Gum		Lamp	22	19	$38	$48						
37	B.O.B.		Bibs	75	53	$9	$12						
38													
39				Baby Gym	Bubble Gum	B.O.B.							
40	Total Markdowns$												
41	Markdown Cancellation$												
42	Net Markdown$												
43	Total Net Markdown$												

Sheet1 / Sheet2 / Sheet3 /

Ready   CAPS NUM

FIGURE 4.1

☀ HINT   This time, you are going to copy the formula into cells **E8**, **E9**, **E12**, and **E13**. Because the percent formula calls for each of these dollar amounts to be divided by net sales, you will need the numerator (e.g., cash discounts) to adjust while the denominator (**D7**, which is the net sales figure) remains constant or absolute.

5. Copy the formula written in cell **E11** into cells **E8, E9, E12,** and **E13**. When this process is complete, the top of your screen should resemble Figure 4.2.

6. Write the formula to calculate gross cost of merchandise sold in cell **D14**: =(D22+D8+D9)-D26.

FIGURE 4.2

	A	B	C	D	E	F	G	H	I	J
1										
2										
3				UPSIDE DOWN SHOP						
4				FALL SEASON						
5	The Upside Down Shop had the following operational results for the fall season:									
6				$	%					
7	Net Sales			$75,000	100.00%					
8	Billed Cost of New Purchases			$36,000	48.00%					
9	Freight			$610	0.81%					
10	Workroom Costs			$120	0.16%					
11	Cash Discounts			$1,080	1.44%					
12	Markdowns			$9,200	12.27%					
13	Shortages			$840	1.12%					
14	Gross Cost of Merchandise Sold									
15	Total Cost of Merchandise Sold									
16						$	%			
17			Maintained Markup							
18			Gross Margin							
19										
20										
21										
22										
23										
24										
25										
26										
27										
28										
29										
30										
31										
32										
33										

☀ HINT   Remember the formula:

> Gross cost of merchandise sold = Opening inventory + New purchases + Freight − Closing inventory

You can find the opening and closing inventory levels listed in rows **22** and **26**, respectively.

7. Write the formula to calculate total cost of merchandise sold in cell **D15**: =D14-D11+D10.

☀ HINT   Remember the formula:

> Total cost of merchandise sold = Gross cost of merchandise sold − Cash discounts earned + Workroom costs

8. Write the formula to calculate maintained markup$ in cell **F17**. Your formula should read: =D7-D14.

☀ HINT   Remember the formula:

> Maintained markup = Net sales − Gross cost of merchandise sold

9. Write the formula to calculate maintained markup% in cell **G17**. This can be accomplished by dividing maintained markup$ by net sales$ or =F17/D7.
10. Write the formula to calculate gross margin$ in cell **F18**. Your formula should read: =D7-D15.

☼ HINT   Remember that **Gross margin** = **Net sales** − **Total cost of merchandise sold**

---

11. Write the formula to calculate gross margin% in cell **G18**. This can be accomplished by dividing gross margin$ by net sales$ or =**F18/D7**.

12. Calculate the markup% obtained on the September 1 shipment. In cell **F23** write the formula to calculate the markup% achieved on the purchase of Baby Gym apparel. As you will remember from previous chapters, the formula should read: =**(E23-D23)/E23**.

13. Copy the formula entered in cell **F23** into cells **F24** and **F25** to obtain markup% for the Bubble Gum and B.O.B. shipments. You can perform this operation more quickly by clicking on the cell you wish to copy (**F23**) and then selecting the **Copy** tool in the toolbar or choosing **Edit** and then **Copy** as you learned in Chapter 1.

14. Write the formula for total $cost of beginning inventory and all new purchases in cell **H25** by typing: =**D22+D23+D24+D25**.

15. Write the formula for total $retail of beginning inventory and all new purchases in cell **H26** by typing: =**E22+E23+E24+E25**.

☼ HINT   The totals found in Steps 14 and 15 will help you to calculate cumulative markup% in a later step.

---

16. Find reductions% by placing your cursor in cell **D28** and typing: =**E12+E13**.

☼ HINT   Remember the formula:

Reductions = Markdowns + Shortages + Employee discounts

In this example, the Upside Down Shop doesn't list any employee discounts, so assume none were granted during this time period.

17. Write the formula to calculate initial markup% in cell **D29** by typing: =(G18+E10-E11+D28)/(E7+D28).

☼ HINT

$$\text{Initial markup} = \frac{\text{Gross margin\% + Workroom costs\% − Cash discounts\% + Reductions\%}}{\text{Net sales\% + Reductions\%}}$$

Because many of these components are calculated on your spreadsheet already, you can use the cell where the result of the calculation is placed rather than calculating that component again. For example, reductions% is calculated in cell **D28** so you can use **D28** in your formula rather than adding markup% and shortages% separately into the calculation for initial markup%.

18. Write the formula that will calculate the cumulative markup% for the period in cell **D30**. Your formula should read: =(H26-H25)/H26. Cumulative markup% in this case is calculated using the basic markup formula [(Retail − Cost) ÷ Retail]. However, because this figure represents an average markup over a period of time, you have to utilize the total retail$ of the opening inventory and all new purchases and the total cost$ of the opening inventory and all new purchases. At this point, your screen should resemble Figure 4.3.

19. Write the formula that will allow the Upside Down Shop to calculate the

			Figure4.3.xls						
	A	B	C	D	E	F	G	H	I	J

UPSIDE DOWN SHOP
FALL SEASON

The Upside Down Shop had the following operational results for the fall season:

	$	%
Net Sales	$75,000	100.00%
Billed Cost of New Purchases	$36,000	48.00%
Freight	$610	0.81%
Workroom Costs	$120	0.16%
Cash Discounts	$1,080	1.44%
Markdowns	$9,200	12.27%
Shortages	$840	1.12%
Gross Cost of Merchandise Sold	$44,030	
Total Cost of Merchandise Sold	$43,070	

	$	%
Maintained Markup	$30,970	41.29%
Gross Margin	$31,930	42.57%

The store had the following plans for the September 1 shipment:

	$Cost	$Retail	MU%		
Opening Inventory	$72,000	$150,000	52.00%		
Purchases-Baby Gym	$8,900	$17,500	49.14%		
Purchases-Bubble Gum	$6,700	$12,200	45.08%		
Purchases-B.O.B.	$2,900	$6,300	53.97%	Tot. $Cost	$90,500
Closing Inventory	$64,580			Tot. $Retail	$186,000
Reductions%	13.39%				
Initial Markup%	48.22%				
Cumulative Markup%	51.34%				

Sheet1 / Sheet2 / Sheet3 /

Ready   CAPS NUM

FIGURE 4.3

total markdowns$ for Baby Gym layettes during the Labor Day Sale in cell **D40**. Your formula should read: =**PRODUCT(D35,(G35-F35))**. This will take the total number of layettes in stock and multiply them by the dollar amount that each layette was reduced for the sale, resulting in total markdown$.

20. Write the formula that will allow the shop to calculate the markdown cancellation$ for Baby Gym layettes during their Labor Day Sale in cell **D41**. Your formula should read: =**PRODUCT ((D35-E35),(G35-F35))**. This formula calculates the number of items left after the sale (Total Items − Number of Items Sold) and multiplies that number by the amount each item was marked back up (Original Retail Price − Sale Price).

FIGURE 4.4

	A	B	C	D	E	F	G	H	I	J	K	L	M
1													
2													
3				UPSIDE DOWN SHOP									
4				FALL SEASON									
5	The Upside Down Shop had the following operational results for the fall season:												
6				$	%								
7	Net Sales			$75,000	100.00%								
8	Billed Cost of New Purchases			$36,000	48.00%								
9	Freight			$610	0.81%								
10	Workroom Costs			$120	0.16%								
11	Cash Discounts			$1,080	1.44%								
12	Markdowns			$9,200	12.27%								
13	Shortages			$840	1.12%								
14	Gross Cost of Merchandise Sold			$44,030									
15	Total Cost of Merchandise Sold			$43,070									
16							$	%					
17			Maintained Markup				$30,970	41.29%					
18			Gross Margin				$31,930	42.57%					
19													
20	The store had the following plans for the September 1 shipment:												
21				$Cost	$Retail	MU%							
22	Opening Inventory			$72,000	$150,000	52.00%							
23	Purchases-Baby Gym			$8,900	$17,500	49.14%							
24	Purchases-Bubble Gum			$6,700	$12,200	45.08%							
25	Purchases-B.O.B.			$2,900	$6,300	53.97%	Tot. $Cost	$90,500					
26	Closing Inventory			$64,580			Tot. $Retail	$186,000					
27													
28	Reductions%			13.39%									
29	Initial Markup%			48.22%									
30	Cumulative Markup%			51.34%									
31													
32	During the Labor Day Sale, the sales data indicated the following results:												
33													
34	Vendor		Item	#In Stock	# Sold	Sales Price	Original Retail						
35	Baby Gym		Layette	50	38	$20	$25						
36	Bubble Gum		Lamp	22	19	$38	$48						
37	B.O.B.		Bibs	75	53	$9	$12						
38													
39				Baby Gym	Bubble Gum	B.O.B.							
40	Total Markdowns$			$250	$220	$225							
41	Markdown Cancellation$			$60	$30	$66							
42	Net Markdown$			$190	$190	$159							
43	Total Net Markdown$			$539									
44													

Sheet1 / Sheet2 / Sheet3 /

☀ HINT In this example, we assumed that the items were returned to their original retail price after the sale. What if, for example, the items originally retailed for $25 and during the sale were offered at $20. After the sale was over, the remaining items were only marked back up to $22. Then your formula would read:

Markdown cancellation$ = (50 layettes − 38 sold) × ($22 − $20)

21. Write the formula in cell **D42** to calculate the net markdown$ for Baby Gym layettes during the Labor Day Sale. Your formula will read: **=D40-D41** because

Net markdown = Total markdown − Markdown cancellations

22. Find the total markdowns$, markdown cancellation$, and net markdown$ for Bubble Gum lamps and B.O.B. bibs during the sale. Make sure your calculations are in the appropriate cells. Format the cells for currency.
23. Write the formula in cell **D43** to total the net markdown$ for the three vendors during the Labor Day Sale. Your formula should read: **=D42+E42+F42.**
24. Your screen should resemble Figure 4.4.

Setting a Print Area and Formatting the Page

25. Set the area of the spreadsheet that you would like to print. Click on cell **A1** and highlight down to cell **H43**. Then select **File** from the menu bar and click on **Print Area/Set Print Area**.
26. Next, select **File** again and this time click on the **Page Setup** option. Select the tab labeled **Sheet**. Turn off the gridlines and row/column headings.
27. Check over your work one last time to ensure that the font size and style is consistent and that the printed work will look professional.

Saving Your Work and Printing

28. Save your work and label it **Lesson4**(your initials here with no spaces).

Printing Formulas

29. Your instructor may request that you also print out your spreadsheet assignment showing all the formulas you have written.

PRACTICE PROBLEMS

Practice Problem 4.1

Open a blank Excel spreadsheet. Save it as **Practice4.1**(your initials here with no spaces).

Create two tables that will allow you to calculate the following:

- An accessories buyer has an opening stock figure of $230,000, at retail. The inventory carries a 51% markup. On August 31, new purchases for the month amounted to $250,000 at retail with a 54% markup. What is the cumulative markup% to date?
- During the spring season, a shoe department determined that the amount of merchandise needed to meet the planned sales was $175,000, at retail with a 52% markup. At the beginning of the season, the merchandise on hand came to $68,000, at retail with a markup of 50%. What initial markup does the buyer need to achieve on any new purchases?

✿ HINT   Be sure to give each column and row a proper heading in order to present your work more professionally.

Save and print your work.

Practice Problem 4.2

Open a blank Excel spreadsheet. Save it as **Practice4.2**(your initials here with no spaces).

Create a table to calculate the initial markup%, reductions%, and maintained markup% for each of the following problems:

- A buyer plans an initial markup of 52% and reductions of 11%. What maintained markup can the buyer expect?
- A shoe department has a planned initial markup of 50%. The manager expects markdowns of 12% and shortages of 2%. The department does not have an employee discount program. What maintained markup can the department expect?
- A junior department has the following figures for the holiday season: Initial markup of 49.5%, employee discounts of 3%, markdowns at 9%, and shortages of 1.5%. What maintained markup can the department expect?
- A buyer plans an initial markup of 48.3% and reductions of 12%. What maintained markup can the buyer expect?

Select a different area on the same spreadsheet page and create a table for the following problem. Calculate the gross cost of merchandise, total cost of merchandise, gross margin%, and maintained markup% for the following example:

Net sales = $789,000
Cost of goods sold = $177,000
New purchases = $385,000
Inward freight = $9,000
Cash discounts = $18,000
Alterations/Workroom = $3,800
Closing inventory = $160,000

☼ HINT   You may want to place a border around each of the two tables in order to present your work more clearly and professionally.

Save and print your work.

Practice Problem 4.3

Open a blank Excel spreadsheet. Save it as **Practice4.3**(your initials here with no spaces).

The owner of Circus Shoe Boutique is considering opening a new location in the retail space adjacent to the Upside Down Shop. As a part of his research, the owner, Steve Patrick, would like to analyze the information given below to determine whether the new location is viable with regard to sales and profit. You will need to provide one spreadsheet (which may contain separate tables) that provides the appropriate analysis to answer Mr. Patrick's questions.

From his openings of previous locations of Circus Shoe Boutique and years in the shoe business, Mr. Patrick knows that the new location will need to achieve a gross margin minimum of 48%. Given the expected costs related to obtaining an opening inventory listed below, what net sales will

Circus Shoe Boutique need to achieve to allow for a 48% gross margin? What gross margin$ will this result in?

Cost of goods		20%
New purchases (Opening	$81,000	60%
inventory for grand opening)		
Inward freight		2%
Closing inventory		25%
Cash discounts		6%
Alterations/Workroom		1%

Mr. Patrick has estimated the following reductions and would like to determine what initial markup would be necessary in the proposed location.

Markdowns	$25,000.00
Employee discounts	$1,200.00
Shortages	$675.00

Because maintained markup is the markup actually achieved on the sale of merchandise, Mr. Patrick would also like to see the maintained markup possible given the estimated figures above. Provide a small chart that depicts the figures you will need to use to calculate maintained markup as well as providing the calculation of maintained markup% and maintained markup$.

Make sure your work addresses Mr. Patrick's concerns in an easy-to-read format. Save and print your work.

☼ HINT   You can use your text and/or previous lessons if you should need to refresh
          your memory of formulas or formatting techniques.

Practice Problem 4.4

Open a blank Excel spreadsheet. Save it as **Practice4.4**(your initials here
with no spaces).

A buyer for the lingerie department at Selby's Department Store has
recorded the following figures:

Gross margin = 46.0%
Markdowns = 9.8%
Employee discounts = 1.5%
Cash discounts = 4.0%
Alteration costs = 0.8%

Create a table that lists the figures given and determines the initial
markup percentage.

After calculating the initial markup, the buyer sets out to determine the
cumulative markup on the merchandise handled in her department to
date. She would like to present this information to the DMM at tomorrow's
executive meeting.

Opening stock	$180,000	52%
New purchases	$335,000	48%

Create a table that lists the figures given and determines the cumulative
markup achieved on merchandise handled.

Save and print your work.

Practice Problem 4.5

Open a blank Excel spreadsheet. Save it as **Practice4.5**(your initials here with no spaces).

   In preparation for a buying trip, a children's buyer determines that a 52% markup is required on purchases to meet expectations for the period. Her total purchases will amount to $750,000 at retail. While on the trip, she made purchases from three vendors as follows:

	COST	RETAIL
Resource A	$50,000	$110,000
Resource B	$15,000	$28,000
Resource C	$75,000	$150,000

   Create a table that depicts the purchases already acquired and indicates the markup percentage needed on the balance of the purchases to achieve the desired cumulative markup.

   Save and print your work.

Practice Problem 4.6

Open a blank Excel spreadsheet. Save it as **Practice4.6**(your initials here with no spaces).

   An infant's buyer operates on a 53% markup and needs 300 layettes that will retail at $18.00 each and 400 blankets that will retail at $12.00 each. If the buyer pays $9.75 for the layettes, create a chart that represents the given information and how much can be spent for each blanket to attain the desired markup on the total purchase.

   Save and print your work.

5 THE RETAIL METHOD OF INVENTORY

A book inventory indicates the retail value of stock that has been determined from records. The physical inventory, in contrast, is an actual count of stock on hand at any given time (usually the end of the period) valued at retail. In this lesson, you will learn to utilize the retail method of inventory to determine the book inventory and shortage/overage.

The retail method begins with a complete physical count of all the goods on hand. The retail value obtained is used as the opening book inventory. Inventory is then reported on the books by taking into account all of those transactions that add to the retail value of the inventory (ins) and those that subtract from the retail value of the inventory (outs).

Once the period is complete, another physical count of the inventory will occur. The difference between the book inventory and the actual physical inventory is stated in terms of shortage or overage. If the physical inventory is less than the book inventory indicates it should be, then a shortage has occurred. If the physical inventory is greater than the books indicate it should be, then an overage has occurred.

INCREASE RETAIL VALUE (INS)	DECREASE RETAIL VALUE (OUTS)
Purchases at retail	Gross sales
Additional markup	Net sales
Transfers in	Transfers out
Freight	Returns to vendor
Customer returns	Employee discounts
Markdown cancellations	Markdowns

FORMULAS

Retail book inventory = Opening inventory + Additions (Ins) − Deductions (Outs)

Book inventory at cost = Retail book inventory × (100% − Markup%)

Shortage (or Overage) = Closing book inventory at retail − Physical inventory

LESSON 5 IMPLEMENTING THE RETAIL METHOD OF INVENTORY

1. Open Excel. From the **File** menu, click **Open** and then locate the file **Lesson5.xls**. Open this file by double clicking on the file name. Your screen should resemble Figure 5.1.

2. Use file **Lesson5.xls** to perform the following tasks:

Completing the Spreadsheet

3. Given the following scenario, calculate the retail book inventory and shortage/overage for the period:

On January 31, the physical inventory count in the men's shirt department at Greenhill's totaled $45,000. On February 1, the opening retail inventory of this department was $45,000. From February 1 to May 31 retail purchases amounted to $79,000 and were received into stock. Net sales during

FIGURE 5.1

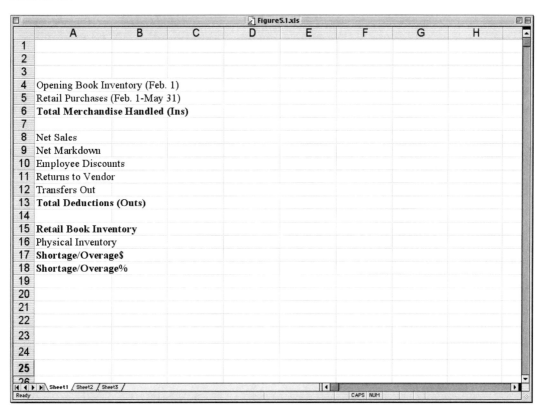

this period were $51,000 and markdowns of $4,700 were taken. Employee discounts amounted to $1,200 and $350 in merchandise was returned to the vendor. Another $500 in merchandise was sent to the Shorthill's store during the period at the request of the Divisional Merchandise Manager. A physical count of the inventory in the store on May 31 revealed merchandise valued at $65,500 at retail.

4. Enter the data given for additions to retail value (ins) into the spreadsheet. Place the figure for opening inventory at retail in cell **D4**. Type the number as 45,000. You will format these figures as **Currency** in a later step. Complete the data entry for additions to retail inventory (ins) by placing 79,000 in cell **D5** to represent retail purchases.

5. Total the additions to retail inventory by placing your cursor in cell **D6** and pressing the **Autosum (Σ)** button in the toolbar. A formula will appear at your cursor: =SUM(D4:D5). Because this formula is correct, press **Enter** or click on the green check mark (✔) in the formula bar.

6. Enter the data given for deductions from retail value (outs) into the spreadsheet. Place the figure for Net Sales into cell **D8**. Type the number as 51,000. You will be asked to format these figures as **Currency** in a later step. Complete the data entry for deductions from retail inventory (outs) by entering in the remaining variables in column D of the appropriate rows.

7. Total the deductions to retail inventory by placing your cursor in cell **D13**. As in Step 5, press the **Autosum (Σ)** button in the toolbar. A flashing dotted line will appear around cells **D8** through **D12**. Because this formula is correct, press **Enter** or click on the green check mark (✔) in the formula bar.

☼ HINT   The figures you entered are not formatted as **Currency**. Highlight cells **D4** through **D17** and format the highlighted figures as **Currency** as instructed in previous lessons. Your screen should resemble Figure 5.2.

	A	B	C	D	E	F	G	H
1								
2								
3								
4	Opening Book Inventory (Feb. 1)			$45,000				
5	Retail Purchases (Feb. 1-May 31)			$79,000				
6	**Total Merchandise Handled (Ins)**			$124,000				
7								
8	Net Sales			$51,000				
9	Net Markdown			$4,700				
10	Employee Discounts			$1,200				
11	Returns to Vendor			$350				
12	Transfers Out			$500				
13	**Total Deductions (Outs)**			$57,750				
14								
15	**Retail Book Inventory**							
16	Physical Inventory							
17	**Shortage/Overage$**							
18	**Shortage/Overage%**							
19								
20								
21								
22								
23								
24								
25								

FIGURE 5.2

8. Write the formula in cell **D15** to calculate the retail book inventory. The formula will read: =**D6-D13**.
9. Enter the physical inventory figure in cell **D16**.
10. Write the formula in cell **D17** to calculate the shortage or overage for the men's shirt department. The shortage or overage is calculated by subtracting the physical inventory from the book inventory figure: =**D15-D16**.
11. Write the formula in cell **D18** to calculate the percentage of net sales that the shortage/overage found in Step 10 represents: =**D17/D8**. Remember to format the cell for percentage.

	A	B	C	D	E	F	G	H
1								
2								
3								
4	Opening Book Inventory (Feb. 1)			$45,000				
5	Retail Purchases (Feb. 1-May 31)			$79,000				
6	**Total Merchandise Handled (Ins)**			$124,000				
7								
8	Net Sales			$51,000				
9	Net Markdown			$4,700				
10	Employee Discounts			$1,200				
11	Returns to Vendor			$350				
12	Transfers Out			$500				
13	**Total Deductions (Outs)**			$57,750				
14								
15	**Retail Book Inventory**			$66,250				
16	Physical Inventory			$65,500				
17	**Shortage/Overage$**			$750				
18	**Shortage/Overage%**			1.47%				
19								
20								
21								
22								
23								
24								
25								
26								

FIGURE 5.3

☼ HINT   You can double-check your work. See Figure 5.3.

Setting a Print Area and Formatting the Page

12. Set the area of the spreadsheet that you would like to print. Click on cell **A1** and highlight down to cell **E18**. Then select **File** from the menu bar and click on **Print Area/Set Print Area**.

13. Next, select **File** again and this time click on the **Page Setup** option. Select the tab labeled **Sheet**. Turn off the gridlines and row/column headings. Select **Print Preview** to see how your spreadsheet will look when printed.
14. When you are through previewing the page, choose **Close** to take you back to your working spreadsheet.

Saving Your Work and Printing

15. Save your work on your diskette and label it **Lesson5**(your initials here with no spaces).

Printing Formulas

16. Your instructor may request that you also print out your spreadsheet assignment showing all the formulas you have written.

PRACTICE PROBLEMS

Practice Problem 5.1

Open a blank Excel spreadsheet. Save it as **Practice5.1**(your initials here with no spaces).

Determine the book inventory and shortage/overage in dollars and percents given the following:

Physical inventory = $69,900
Opening inventory = $72,700
Gross sales = $36,900

Employee discounts = $475
Purchases = $26,600
Markup cancellations = $975
Additional markup = $1,100
Markdown cancellation = $800
Returns to vendor = $1,500
Customer returns = $9,800
Markdowns = $1,050

Save and print your work.

Practice Problem 5.2

Open a blank Excel spreadsheet. Save it as **Practice5.2**(your initials here with no spaces).

The figures below are from a junior sportswear department. Determine the closing book inventory for the period.

Markdowns = $9,000
Purchases = $275,000
Returns to vendor (RTVs) = $17,000
Transfers in = $6,500
Transfers out = $2,800
Net sales = $232,000
Opening book inventory = $165,000

Save and print your work.

Practice Problem 5.3

Open a blank Excel spreadsheet. Save it as **Practice5.3**(your initials here with no spaces).

A costume jewelry department had the following figures for a four-month period:

Net sales = $110,000
Purchases = $95,000
Opening inventory = $60,000
Markdowns = $7,000
Employee discounts = $1,300
Physical count = $24,700
Markup on total merchandise handled = 48.5%

Create a spreadsheet that includes all the data listed above and allows you to calculate:

- Book inventory at retail
- Book inventory at cost [**HINT: Cost** = Retail × (100% − MU%)]
- Shortage/Overage dollars and percent

Save and print your work.

Practice Problem 5.4

Open a blank Excel spreadsheet. Save it as **Practice5.4**(your initials here with no spaces).

The furniture department at Parkinson's Department Store recorded the following figures. Complete a spreadsheet that determines the closing inventory at cost.

	COST	RETAIL
Net sales		$350,000
Opening inventory	$175,000	$340,000
Markdowns		$38,000
RTVs	$14,000	$19,000
Employee discounts		$8,000
Gross purchases	$180,000	$325,000

Save and print your work.

☼ HINT You can use your text and/or previous lessons if you should need to refresh your memory of formulas or formatting techniques.

Practice Problem 5.5

Open a blank Excel spreadsheet. Save it as **Practice5.5**(your initials here with no spaces).

  Create a chart that determines the book inventory and shortage/overage in dollars and percentages given the following information for the lingerie department:

Physical inventory = $189,900
Opening inventory = $235,000
Gross sales = $225,000
Employee discounts = $975
Purchases = $165,000
Additional markup = $1,100

Markdown cancellation = $1,800
Returns to vendor = $1,500
Customer returns = $18,000
Markdowns = $19,000

If the markup% for the lingerie department is 51%, calculate the closing book inventory at cost and add it to the chart created in Step 2.

Save and print your work.

Practice Problem 5.6

Open a blank Excel spreadsheet. Save it as **Practice5.6**(your initials here with no spaces).

A men's outerwear department had an opening inventory of $275,000. The net purchases were $55,000, gross sales were $105,500, customer returns were $8,500, and markdowns were $2,500. Shortages were estimated at 2%. Create a chart that depicts the information given and calculates the following:

- Closing retail book inventory
- Estimated physical inventory

Save and print your work.

6

DOLLAR PLANNING AND CONTROL

The six-month seasonal merchandise plan represents the retailers' efforts to maintain proper proportion between sales, inventories, and prices to turn a profit. The inventory levels should reflect customer demand while remaining consistent with the financial limits set by management. In this lesson, you will learn to plan sales, stock, markdowns, and purchases as well as to determine gross margin and stock turn.

FORMULAS

$$\text{Sales\% increase} = \frac{(\text{TY planned sales} - \text{LY planned sales})}{\text{LY planned sales}}$$

Seasonal planned sales = LY sales $\times$ Planned% increase

Gross margin = Expenses + Profit
  OR
Gross margin = IM% $-$ (MD% and Shrink% at Cost) $-$ (CD% and Alterations%)

$$\text{Turnover} = \frac{\text{Net sales}}{\text{Average stock}}$$

$$\text{Average stock} = \frac{\text{Net sales}}{\text{Turnover}}$$

OR

$$\text{Average stock} = \frac{(\text{Beginning inventories} + \text{Ending inventory for the period})}{\text{Number of inventories}}$$

$$\text{Stock-sales ratio} = \frac{\text{BOM stock}}{\text{Sales (usually calculated for each month)}}$$

$$\text{BOM stock} = \text{Planned monthly sales} \times \text{Stock-sales ratio}$$

$$\text{Basic stock} = \text{Average inventory} - \text{Average monthly sales}$$

$$\text{Average inventory} = \frac{\text{Sales}}{\text{Stock turn}}$$

$$\text{Average monthly sales} = \frac{\text{Sales for the period}}{\text{Number of months (usually 6)}}$$

$$\text{Planned purchases (receipts)} = \text{Sales} + \text{Markdowns} + \text{EOM} - \text{BOM}$$

$$\text{Planned purchases at cost} = \text{Planned purchases at retail} \times (100\% - \text{Planned markup\%})$$

LESSON 6 SIX-MONTH SEASONAL DOLLAR PLAN

Opening the File

1. Open Excel. From the **File** menu, click **Open** and then locate the file entitled **Lesson6.xls.** You can open this file by double clicking on the file ame. Your screen should resemble Figure 6.1.

2. Use file **Lesson6.xls** to perform the following tasks:

Completing the Spreadsheet

3. Given the information for last year, plan a 6% increase and complete the six-month plan. Enter the formula in cell **K16** to calculate a 6% increase in total sales for TY (this year). Your formula should read: **=K15*1.06**. This

FIGURE 6.1

	A	B	C	D	E	F	G	H	I	J	K	L	M
										Planning and Authorization			
5									Buyer_____				
7									Merchandise				
8									Manager_____				
9									Date Authorized_____				
12					Six-Month Merchandise Plan								
13	Six-Month Merchandise Plan			Spring	February	March	April	May	June	July	Total		
14	Department Name_____			Fall	August	September	October	November	December	January		Avg Stock	
15	From: February 1			LY Sales$	$110,000	$140,000	$110,000	$150,000	$130,000	$150,000	$790,000		
16	To: July 31			TY Plan									
17	Department Financial Data			Actual									
18		LY	TY Plan	LY BOM$	$200,000	$218,150	$193,930	$194,970	$173,380	$192,050			
19				Stock/Sales Ratio									
20	Initial MU%	53.0%	53.0%	TY Plan								$196,500	
21	Markdown%	15.0%	15.0%	Actual									
22	Shrinkage%	2.7%	2.0%	LY Receipts$	$140,000	$130,000	$130,000	$145,000	$170,000	$125,000	$840,000		
23	(Workroom Cost)	1.0%	1.0%	TY Plan									
24	(Cash Discount)	____	____	Actual									
25	(Gross Margin)	43.2%	____	LY Markdown$	$11,850	$14,220	$18,960	$16,590	$21,330	$35,550	$118,500		
26	Average Stock	$186,283		Monthly MD%									
27	Turnover Rate	4.24		TY Plan									
28				Actual									

formula allows you to encompass all of last year's sales (100%) plus 6% more. When you have finished typing the formula, press **Enter** or click on the green check mark (✔) in the formula bar.

☀ HINT   Don't worry about the format of the numbers at this point. You will be asked to format these cells in a later step.

---

4. Write the formula in cell **E16** to calculate the monthly planned sales for February, taking into account last year's sales for the month and this year's planned increase in total sales. You will need to calculate the percentage of last year's total that occurred in February and then multiply that by this year's total planned sales. Your formula should read: **=(E15/$K$15)*$K$16**. (The dollar signs in the formula let the spreadsheet know that those cells are absolute. The reference will not change when the formula is copied.) When you have finished typing the formula, press **Enter** or click on the green check mark (✔) in the formula bar.
5. Copy the formula in cell **E16** into cells **F16** through **J16** to complete this year's monthly sales distribution.

Formatting Planned Sales Figures

6. Place your cursor on cell **E16** and hold down the left mouse button. Drag your cursor to cell **K16** to highlight these cells. Once the cells are highlighted, release the left mouse button. First click on the **Center** alignment button located in the menu bar. Then make sure that your text is **Times New Roman** with a font size of 8. Then click **Format** and select **Cells** from the pull-down menu. Select **Currency** and make sure that the decimal place indicates 0. Your screen should resemble Figure 6.2.

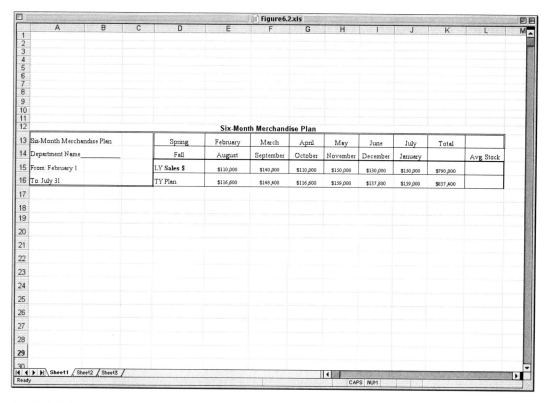

FIGURE 6.2

7. Write the formula in cell **E19** to calculate the stock to sales ratio for the month of February last year. Your formula will read: =E18/E15.

☀ HINT   Once again, we will format these cells in a later step.

---

8. Copy the formula in cell **E19** into cells **F19** through **J19** to complete the stock-sales ratios for the remaining months of the plan.

Formatting the Stock-Sales Ratio Figures

9. Place your cursor in cell **E19** and drag to cell **J19** to highlight. As in Step 6, once the cells are highlighted select **Center** from the alignment buttons and make sure the text is **Times New Roman** with a font size of 8. Then click **Format** and select **Cells** from the pull-down menu. Select **Number** and make sure that the decimal place indicates **2**.
10. Write the formula in cell **E20** to calculate TY plan BOM for February using the stock-sales ratio. Your formula will read: =**E19*E16**. (This formula assumes that the stock to sales ratios will remain the same as last year. Market intelligence may give the buyer reason to believe that these ratios should be adjusted, but for our purposes here we can assume that the ratios will remain unchanged.)
11. Copy the formula in cell **E20** into cells **F20** through **J20** to complete the BOM stock calculations for the remaining months of the plan.

Formatting the BOM Stock Figures

12. Use the stock-sales ratio method by highlighting cells **E20** through **J20**. Once the cells are highlighted, select **Center** from the alignment buttons and make sure the text is **Times New Roman** with a font size of 8. Then click **Format** and select **Cells** from the pull-down menu. Select **Currency** and make sure that the decimal place indicates **0**.

☀ HINT   If any of the numbers appear bold, simply press the **B** button in the menu bar while the cells are highlighted to turn off the bold function.

---

13. Calculate total markdown by placing your cursor in cell **K27**. Markdowns are planned at 15%, just as they were last year. You can calculate the total

dollar markdown amount much as you did the sales increase for this year in Step 1. Your formula should read (=**K25*1.15**) to indicate that you need 100% of last year's sales plus an increase of 15%.

Determining the Percent of Markdowns Monthly

14. When the percentage of markdowns for each month is not specified, we have to base this year's monthly markdowns on last year's allocation. First, determine each monthly markdown amount as a percent of last year's total markdowns. Place your cursor in cell **E26**. Then type the formula that divides last year's February markdowns by last year's total markdown amount (=**E25/$K$25**). Hold the cell in which the total markdowns are entered constant so that it remains the same when you copy the formula for the other months, in cells **F26** through **J26**.

15. Place your cursor on cell **E26**, hold down the left mouse button and drag the cursor to **J26** to highlight the row. Then select **Center** from the alignment buttons and make sure the text is **Times New Roman** with a font size of 8. Then click **Format** and select **Cells** from the pull-down menu. Select **Percentage** and make sure the decimal place indicates 0. Make sure the bold function **B** is not activated.

16. Write the formula to calculate this year's monthly markdowns for February based on last year's percentage of total in cell **E27**. The formula should read [=**(E25/$K$25)*$K$27**]. This formula can then be copied into cells **F27** through **J27**. Make sure the cells are formatted in the proper manner following the instructions in Step 12. At this point, your screen should resemble Figure 6.3.

17. Calculate the monthly receipts (OTB) by writing a formula in cell **E23** (=**E15+E27+F20-E20**). This formula can now be copied into cells **F23** through **I23**. You will be asked to write a formula for July (**J23**) in Step 19. You will need to complete the formatting process for cells **E23** through **I23** just as you did in Step 12.

```
┌─────────────────────────── Figure6.3.xls ────────────────────────────┐
```

	A	B	C	D	E	F	G	H	I	J	K	L	M
1													
2													
3													
4													
5									Planning and Authorization				
6													
7								Buyer_____					
8								Merchandise					
9								Manager_____					
10								Date Authorized_____					
11													
12					Six-Month Merchandise Plan								
13	Six-Month Merchandise Plan			Spring	February	March	April	May	June	July	Total		
14	Department Name_____			Fall	August	September	October	November	December	January		Avg Stock	
15	From: February 1			LY Sales $	$110,000	$140,000	$110,000	$150,000	$130,000	$150,000	$790,000		
16	To: July 31			TY Plan	$116,600	$148,400	$116,600	$159,000	$137,800	$159,000	$837,400		
17	Department Financial Data			Actual									
18		LY	TY Plan	LY BOM$	$200,000	$218,150	$193,930	$194,970	$173,380	$192,050			
19				Stock/Sales Ratio	1.82	1.56	1.76	1.30	1.33	1.28		$196,500	
20	Initial MU%	53.0%	53.0%	TY Plan	$212,000	$231,239	$205,566	$206,668	$183,783	$203,573			
21	Markdown%	15.0%	15.0%	Actual									
22	Shrinkage%	2.7%	2.0%	LY Receipts $	$140,000	$130,000	$130,000	$145,000	$170,000	$125,000	$840,000		
23	(Workroom Cost)	1.0%	1.0%	TY Plan									
24	(Cash Discount)	___	___	Actual									
25	(Gross Margin)	43.2%	___	LY Markdown $	$11,850	$14,220	$18,960	$16,590	$21,330	$35,550	$118,500		
26	Average Stock	$186,283		Monthly MD%	10%	12%	16%	14%	18%	30%			
27	Turnover Rate	4.24		TY Plan	$13,628	$16,353	$21,804	$19,079	$24,530	$40,883	$136,275		
28				Actual									
29													
30													

```
│◄ ◄ ► ►│\ Sheet1 / Sheet2 / Sheet3 /              │◄ ▥                    ►│
│ Ready                                                    CAPS  NUM         │
```

FIGURE 6.3

☀ HINT   When a column is not wide enough to hold the value entered, it is possible that you will see "#####" in the cell. Format the cell as directed and the correct figure will appear. In some instances, you may need to widen the column by pointing your cursor at the column-heading letter on the right sideline of the column. When in position, your cursor will turn from a single pointer arrow to a cross with a left and right arrow pointing. When you see the symbol, hold the left mouse button down and drag the column sideline to your chosen width.

18. Write the formula to calculate **average stock** (aka **average inventory**) in cell **C26**. This can be done by averaging all the BOM stock figures and the end-of-season stock figure (EOS). Your formula should read: **=(E20+F20+G20+H20+I20+J20+L20)/7**.

19. Calculate July receipts (OTB) for the spreadsheet. In Step 17, you will notice that the EOM stock figure necessary to complete the open-to-buy formula (OTB) is equal to the BOM stock figure for the next month. For July, however, use the *average stock* figure as the EOM figure because there is no BOM figure for August. Your formula in cell **J23** should read: **=J16+J27+L20-J20**.

20. Write the formula in cell **C27** to calculate the turnover for this year. Place your cursor in cell **C27** and then write **=K16/L20**.

☼ HINT   Remember that turnover (stockturn) is defined as the number of times that average stock turns into net sales. Your screen should now resemble Figure 6.4.

Setting a Print Area and Formatting the Page

21. Set the area of the spreadsheet that you would like to print. Click on cell **A1** and highlight down to cell **L28**. Then select **File** from the menu bar and click on **Print Area/Set Print Area**.

22. Next, select **File** again and this time click on the **Page Setup** option. Select the tab labeled **Sheet**. Turn off the gridlines and row/column headings. You can select **Print Preview** to see how your spreadsheet will look when printed.

23. When you are through previewing the page, choose **Close** to take you back to your working spreadsheet.

Figure6.4.xls

Planning and Authorization

Buyer____
Merchandise
Manager____
Date Authorized____

Six-Month Merchandise Plan

	LY	TY Plan		Spring	February	March	April	May	June	July	Total	Avg Stock
Six-Month Merchandise Plan				Fall	August	September	October	November	December	January		Avg Stock
Department Name____			LY Sales$		$110,000	$140,000	$110,000	$150,000	$130,000	$150,000	$790,000	
From: February 1			TY Plan		$116,600	$148,400	$116,600	$159,000	$137,800	$159,000	$837,400	
To: July 31			Actual									
Department Financial Data			LY BOM$		$200,000	$218,150	$193,930	$194,970	$173,380	$192,050		
	LY	TY Plan	Stock/Sales Ratio		1.82	1.56	1.76	1.30	1.33	1.28		$196,500
Initial MU%	53.0%	53.0%	TY Plan		$212,000	$231,239	$205,566	$206,668	$183,783	$203,573		
Markdown%	15.0%	15.0%	Actual									
Shrinkage%	2.7%	2.0%	LY Receipts$		$140,000	$130,000	$130,000	$145,000	$170,000	$125,000	$840,000	
(Workroom Cost)	1.0%	1.0%	TY Plan		$142,867	$130,680	$132,906	$146,193	$174,320	$192,810		
(Cash Discount)	—	—	Actual									
(Gross Margin)	43.2%		LY Markdown$		$11,850	$14,220	$18,960	$16,590	$21,330	$35,550	$118,500	
Average Stock	$186,283	$205,618	Monthly MD%		10%	12%	16%	14%	18%	30%		
Turnover Rate	4.24	4.26	TY Plan		$13,628	$16,353	$21,804	$19,079	$24,530	$40,883	$136,275	
			Actual									

Sheet1 / Sheet2 / Sheet3 /

Ready CAPS NUM

FIGURE 6.4

Saving Your Work and Printing

24. Save your work on your diskette and label it **Lesson6**(your initials here with no spaces).
25. Print out the final results as directed by your instructor.

Printing Formulas

26. Your instructor may request that you also print out your spreadsheet

assignment showing all the formulas you have written. Refer to Chapter 1 for instructions if necessary.

PRACTICE PROBLEMS

Practice Problem 6.1

Open the Excel spreadsheet **Practice6.1.xls**. Your screen should resemble Figure 6.5. Save it as **Practice6.1**(your initials here with no spaces).

FIGURE 6.5

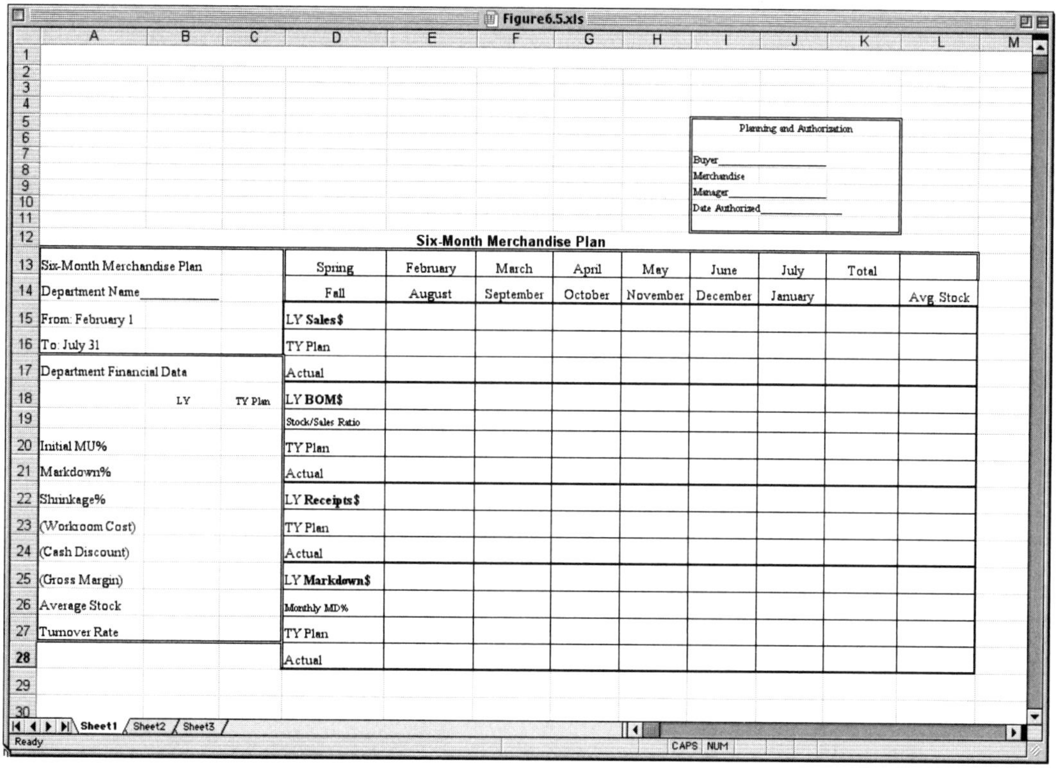

In Lesson 6, you completed a six-month merchandise plan using the stock-sales ratio to plan BOM stock levels. Use the following data to complete the blank spreadsheet using the basic stock method for planning BOM stock levels.

The men's sportswear department has planned sales for this year of $420,000. Monthly sales are planned as follows:

February = 14%
March = 16%
April = 20%
May = 20%
June = 16%
July = 14%

Markdowns are planned for 12% for the season and are allocated as follows:

February = 15%
March = 18%
April = 20%
May = 17%
June = 15%
July = 15%

Turnover is expected to remain similar to last year at 3.6. Make sure your spreadsheet includes completed planned monthly sales, planned BOM stock levels, planned monthly markdowns, planned monthly receipts, average stock, and turnover rate.

Save and print your work.

☼ HINT You will need this figure to complete the BOM stocks using the basic stock method. Refer to the *Mathematics for Retail Buying* text if you have trouble remembering the formula.

Practice Problem 6.2

Open the Excel spreadsheet **Practice6.2**. Your screen should resemble Figure 6.4. Save it as **Practice6.2**(your initials).

You recently completed this six-month seasonal merchandise plan. When you presented your plan to the Divisional Merchandise Manager, she indicated that with the recent downturn in the economy, she felt the following changes should be made:

- Instead of a 6% increase, you and she agree that a 4% increase may be a more realistic goal.
- She also expects the overall markdown percentages to increase by 2%.
- You also realize during your discussion that Easter will fall at the end of March this year rather than in April as it did last year. Because your department runs a big Easter sale every year two weeks prior to the holiday, you will need to change the markdown% for March to the percentage you had allocated to April last year (the percentage for April will be allocated to March).

Save and print your work. Your instructor may want you to complete Practice Problem 6.6 along with this assignment. Be sure to ask before shutting down your computer and turning in your work.

Practice Problem 6.3

Open the Excel spreadsheet **Practice6.2**(your initials). Save the file as **Practice6.3**(your initials).

For this exercise, you are going to be able to compare the BOM stock levels using the basic stock method to those obtained using the stock-sales ratio method. Given the following stock-sales ratios for each month, calculate the BOM stock levels in the example using the stock-sales ratio method (replacing those figures obtained using the basic stock method):

February = 2.0
March = 2.3
April = 2.8
May = 3.0
June = 2.5
July = 2.0

Be sure to save your work. Print out the files **Practice6.1**(your initials), **Practice6.2**(your initials), and **Practice6.3**(your initials). Compare the files and write a brief summary of the significant differences. Type the information and use bullet points to present the information. Staple all three printouts together to submit to the instructor.

Practice Problem 6.4

Open a blank Excel spreadsheet. Save it as **Practice6.4**(your initials).

Use the figures below for Chad's Card Shop and create a spreadsheet that lists the given figures, yearly average stock figure, the turnover for the year, the turnover for August, and the stock-sales ratio for September.

	BOM STOCKS	NET SALES
January	$25,000	$8,000
February	24,000	7,000
March	24,000	7,600
April	22,000	6,900
May	23,500	7,000
June	23,500	7,500
July	22,000	6,700
August	20,000	6,500
September	22,000	5,900
October	24,000	7,000
November	25,000	7,200
December	20,000	8,800
January	19,500	

Save and print your work.

Practice Problem 6.5

Open the Excel spreadsheet **Lesson6.1.xls**. Your screen should resemble Figure 6.1. Save it as **Practice6.5**(your initials).

Complete a six-month merchandise plan using the stock-sales ratio to plan BOM stock levels.

February = 2.0
March = 2.3
April = 2.8
May = 2.5
June = 2.5
July = 2.0

Sales estimates total an increase of 6% and monthly sales are planned as follows:

February = 12%
March = 14%
April = 22%
May = 22%
June = 16%
July = 14%

Markdowns are planned for 18% for the season and are allocated as follows:

February = 16%
March = 17%
April = 18%
May = 17%
June = 15%
July = 17%

Turnover is expected to remain similar to last year at 2.3. Make sure your spreadsheet includes completed planned monthly sales, planned BOM stock levels, planned monthly markdowns, planned monthly receipts, average stock, and turnover rate.

Save and print your work.

Practice Problem 6.6

Open the Excel spreadsheet **Practice6.2.xls**(your initials) Save it as **Practice6.6**(your initials).

Your Divisional Merchandise Manager has just pointed out that you forgot to calculate gross margin for this seasonal merchandise plan. Calculate the gross margin for this year given the figures for initial markup, mark-down, shrinkage, cash discounts, and workroom costs.

Save and print your work.

 HINT   You may want to refer to the formulas in your textbook or at the beginning of this chapter to complete this calculation. Remember that to convert a re-tail figure to cost, find the cost complement.

7

INVOICE MATHEMATICS

In this chapter, you will be introduced to the common terms of sale often negotiated in a retail environment. In addition to the cost price negotiated by the buyer, successful negotiation of terms can have a significant impact on the bottom line. The factors discussed in this chapter include discounts, dating, anticipation, and transportation. Each of these can help to lower the cost of goods. We will also briefly practice "loading," which does not change the amount the store actually pays for the merchandise but does allow the store's accounting office to maintain all inventory at the same cash discount rate.

DEFINITIONS

trade discount: A percentage or series of percentages deducted from the list price. These discounts are not dependent on when the invoice is paid. If expressed as a series (for example 40%, 15%, 10%), they must be taken individually and in order. You cannot add these discounts together (for example, a discount of 40%, 15%, 10% is not equivalent to a discount of 65%).

quantity discount: Percentage of the billed cost given when a prearranged quantity of merchandise is purchased. Often used as an incentive to get the buyer to commit to a larger quantity of goods from one vendor.

cash discount: The most common type of discount. Cash discounts are offered as an incentive for the buyer to pay the amount due early. The time frame for taking the cash discount is often dependent on the dating terms agreed upon during the negotiation process.

anticipation: An extra discount sometimes offered as an incentive for the retailer to pay as early as possible in an extended cash discount period. When offered and received, this discount is added to the cash discount and deducted from the billed cost. This is the only time discounts will be added together. For this course, we will use a 6% yearly rate based on a 360-day year.

loading: An adjustment to the cost price of an item to allow for an additional cash discount. A retailer or store may prefer a standard cash discount that is greater than the cash discount being offered by the vendor. The price of the item is adjusted upward (loaded) in order to accommodate the higher cash discount while resulting in the same payment to the vendor. (Loaded cost = Net cost ÷ Complement of the desired cash discount).

COD dating: Cash on delivery. Payment must be rendered in full when the goods are delivered.

regular dating: The cash discount period is calculated from the date of invoice (which is usually the same date that the merchandise is shipped). Example: 2/10, n/30 where a 2% cash discount can be taken if payment is made within 10 days of the date of invoice, otherwise the net amount (payment in full) is due within 30 days of the date of invoice.

extra dating: The cash discount is calculated from the date of invoice but a specific number of extra days are added to the cash discount period. This type of dating can allow the retailer time to receive and even sell some or all of the merchandise before paying for the shipment and receiving the cash discount. Example: 2/10 − 30X where the 2% cash discount period is 10 days plus 30 extra (40 days) from the date of invoice. Otherwise the net (full amount) of the bill is due within 20 days after the last day to take the cash discount. (This is the usual net date, though it is often not stated.)

end of month dating (EOM): A cash discount period offered 10 days from the end of the month in which the merchandise is invoiced. Example: 6/10 EOM where a 6% cash discount is offered 10 days from the end of the month. Traditionally, invoices dated after the 25th of the month allow 10 days from the end of the *following* month.

receipt of goods dating (ROG): The cash discount period is offered for 10 days after the goods are received. In this case, the date of the invoice is not used in the calculation of the discount period.

advanced or postdating: A situation where the vendor actually places a date on the invoice that is some time in the future and then offers regular dating terms. Example: A vendor may ship merchandise on August 1 but place an invoice date on the merchandise of September 1. The vendor then offers 2/10, n/30 from the postdated invoice date, allowing the retailer an extended period of time to take the cash discount.

LESSON 7 TERMS OF SALE AND THE PURCHASE ORDER

Opening the File

1. Open Excel. From the **File** menu, click **Open** and then locate the file entitled **Lesson7.1.xls.** You can open this file by double clicking on the file name. Your screen should resemble Figure 7.1.
2. Use file **Lesson7.xls** to perform the following tasks:

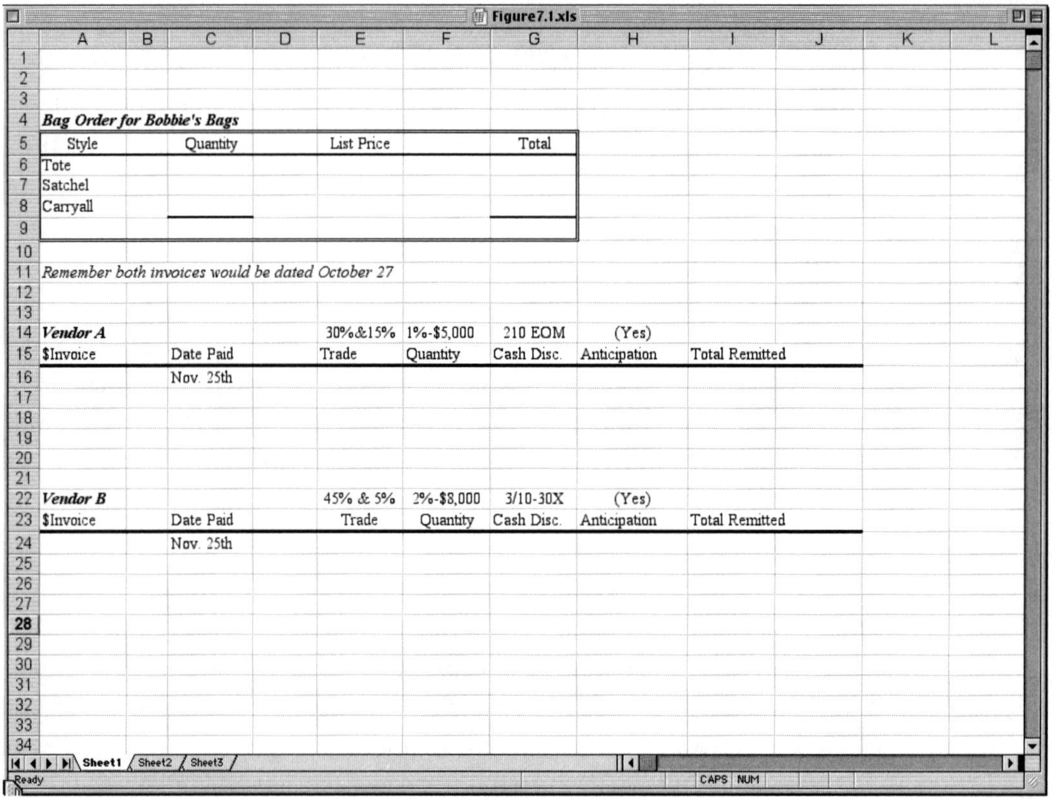

FIGURE 7.1

Completing the Spreadsheet

3. Bobbie's Bags needs to purchase the following shipment of bags:

STYLE	QUANTITY	LIST PRICE
Tote	200	$25.00
Satchel	100	$30.00
Carryall	250	$20.00

4. Each of the vendors shown below is able to provide a suitable product at the same list price. The terms each vendor is offering are listed. Determine the amount that should be remitted to each vendor if payment is made on November 25.

VENDOR A:

- Terms 2/10 EOM
- Invoice dated: October 27
- Anticipation permitted
- Trade discount 30% and 15%
- 1% Quantity discount on orders of $5,000 or more

VENDOR B:

- Terms 3/10-30X
- Invoice dated: October 27
- Anticipation permitted
- Trade discount 45% and 5%
- 2% Quantity discount on orders of $8,000 or more

5. Enter the purchase data in the appropriate cells. Begin by placing the quantities in cells **C6** through **C8**. Next, place the list prices in cells **E6** through **E8**.

6. Format the data entries. Place your cursor in cell **C6**, hold down the left mouse button, and drag down to cell **C8** to highlight the quantity cells. After highlighting, select **Center** from the alignment buttons to center the data in the cells.

7. Format the list price entries. Place your cursor in cell **E6**, hold down the left mouse button, and drag down to cell **E8** to highlight the list price cells. After highlighting, select **Center** from the alignment buttons to center the data in the cells. Make sure the text is **Times New Roman** with a font size of **8**. Then click **Format** and select **Cells** from the pull-down menu. Select **Currency** and make sure that the decimal place indicates **2**.

8. In cell **C9**, calculate the total quantity to be purchased. Place your cursor in that cell and click on the **Autosum (Σ)** symbol located in the formatting bar. The formula reading =**SUM(C6:C8)** will appear in the cell and a flashing box will encircle the cells. Press **Enter** or click on the check mark (✔). While your cursor is still in this cell, click the **Center** alignment button located in the formatting bar to center the total in the cell.

9. Write the formula to calculate the total purchase amount for each style. Begin with the Tote style. Place your cursor in cell **G6** and type =**C6*E6**. You will notice that the amount appears in your cell already formatted in currency format. (If the amount is not properly formatted, use the directions in Step 7 to correct any problems.)

10. Copy the formula in cell **G6** into cells **G7** and **G8**.

11. Calculate the total purchase amount by placing your cursor in cell **G9**. Click on the **Autosum (Σ)** symbol located in the formatting bar. The formula reading =**SUM(G6:G8)** will appear in the cell and a flashing box will encircle the cells. Press **Enter** or click on the check mark (✔).

12. Format the totals figures by highlighting cells **G6** through **G9** and selecting **Center** from the alignment buttons. Also make sure that the font type and size are consistent. Your screen should resemble Figure 7.2.

13. Enter the total purchase amount calculated in cell **G9** into cells **A16** and **A24** (for vendors A and B, respectively). Because copying the formula in that cell will cause the formula to change, it is best to type the amount in each of the cells.

14. Write the formula to calculate the purchase price less the trade discount for Vendor A in cell **E16**: =**(A16*0.7)*0.85**. This formula takes the discounts in order by first multiplying by the complement of the 30% discount and then by the complement of the 15% discount.

15. Write the formula in cell **F16** to deduct the quantity discount of 1% from the newly discounted purchase amount: =**E16*.99**. The total purchase price of the order entitles you to the 1% quantity discount because it surpasses the $5,000 minimum indicated.

16. Determine whether Bobbie's Bags is eligible for a cash discount. The terms

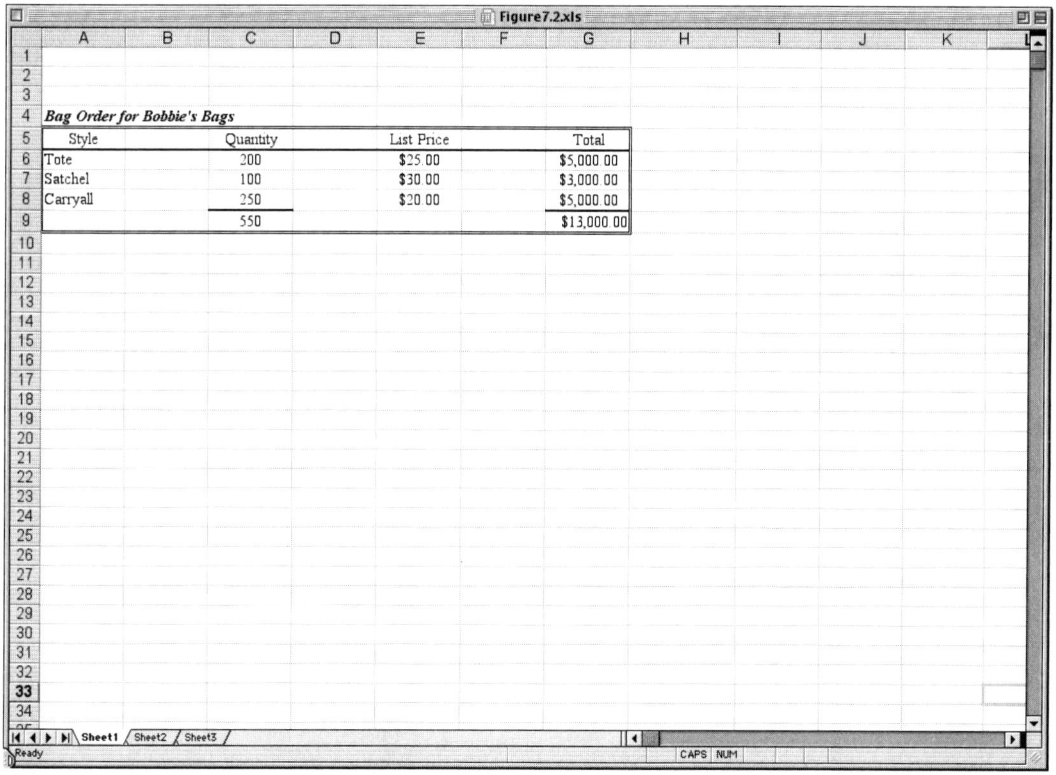

FIGURE 7.2

indicate that a cash discount of 2% can be taken if the invoice is paid within 10 days of the end of the month. In this case, the invoice date is *after the 26th*, so start from the end of November. This gives a cash discount date of December 10. The data indicate a payment date of November 25th, so the cash discount can be taken. Because anticipation is permitted and we are eligible for 16 days of anticipation (6 days remaining in November and 10 days in December), we are going to add the cash and anticipation discount together and deduct them in cell **I16**. For now, type 2% in cell **G16** and .27% in cell **H16**.

☼ HINT   The anticipation rate can be calculated as 16/360 × 6%=.27%. Then add that to the 2% cash discount for a total deduction of 2.27% (the complement of which is 97.73%).

17. Write the formula in cell **I16** to deduct the cash discount and anticipation percentage and yield the amount to be remitted. The formula should read **=F16*(1-(G16+H16))**. The formula could also be written **=F16*.9773**.

☼ HINT   Note that the spreadsheet package will accept two sets of parentheses in a single formula as indicated in this step.

18. Use the terms for trade given for Vendor B to determine the amount necessary for remittance to that vendor.

☼ HINT   You must determine whether Bobbie's Bags is eligible for the cash discount and anticipation with this vendor as well. The terms indicate that a cash discount of 3% can be taken if the invoice is paid within 10 days with 30 extra (a total of 40 days). The invoice date is October 27th so you have:

• 4 remaining days in October
• 30 days in November
• 6 days in December (December 6th is the last day to take the cash discount)

Because the invoice was paid on November 25th, Bobbie's Bags is entitled to the cash discount *plus* 11 days of anticipation (calculated as 11/360 × 6% = .18%).

Setting a Print Area and Formatting the Page

19. Select a border style and set the print area as you have done in previous lessons.
20. Next, eliminate the gridlines and row/column headings.

Saving Your Work and Printing

21. Save your work as **Lesson7**(your initials). Your screen should resemble Figure 7.3 when the steps are complete.

FIGURE 7.3

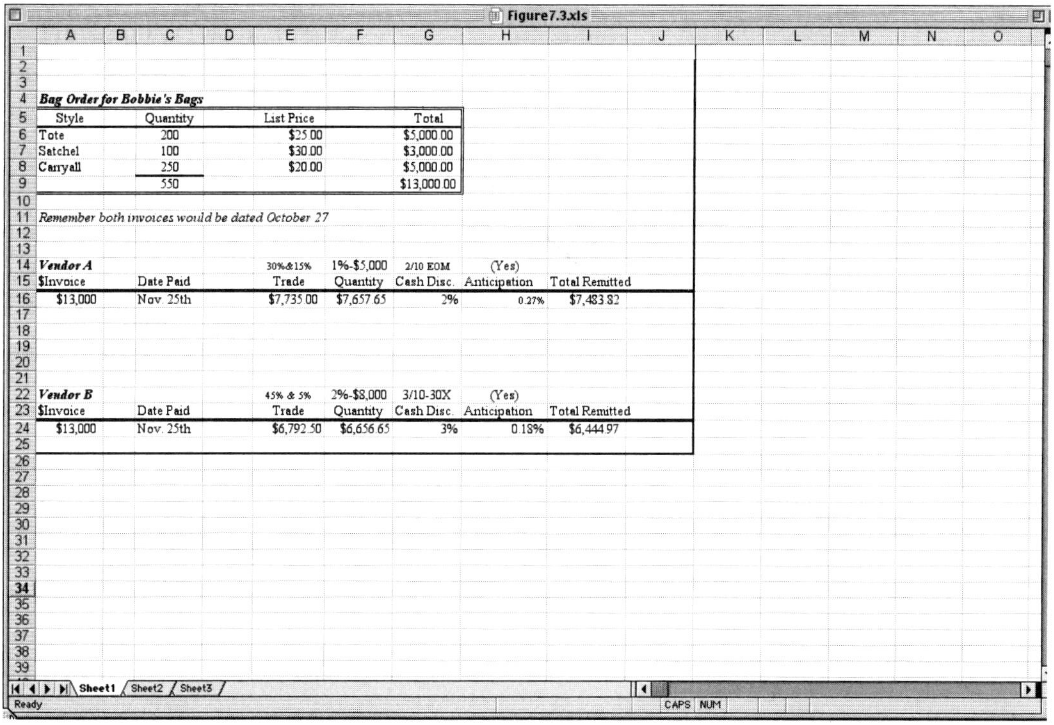

Printing Formulas

22. Your instructor may request that you also print out your spreadsheet assignment showing all the formulas you have written.

PRACTICE PROBLEMS

Practice Problem 7.1

Open a blank Excel spreadsheet. Save it as **Practice7.1**(your initials). Create a table to calculate the loaded cost for the following items:

- A handbag that normally costs $75.00 is sold with a 5% cash discount. If the buyer wants an 8% discount, what would be the loaded cost?
- A blazer that normally costs $86.00 is sold with a 3% cash discount. If the buyer wants a 6% discount, what would be the loaded cost?
- A toaster oven that normally costs $22.00 is sold with a 5% cash discount. If the buyer wants an 8% discount, what would be the loaded cost?
- A costume jewelry buyer purchases a pair of earrings at a cost of $12.00 per pair. The terms normally offered are 1/10, n/30. What would be the loaded cost if the buyer desires 5/10, n/30 terms?

Present the data given and your calculations to represent the results. For instance, you may want a column with the item, cost, cash discount offered, and the cash discount desired, as well as the loaded cost.

Save and print your work.

Practice Problem 7.2

Open a blank Excel spreadsheet. Save it as **Practice7.2**(your initials).
    Create a table depicting the total amount remitted for the following group of items if the trade discount and cash discount are taken.

- The accessories buyer placed an order for the following:
  24 Leather totes at list price $25.00 each
  40 Cell phone cases at list price $10.00 each
  20 Leather card cases at list price $16.00 each
  50 Watches at list price $22.00 each
  20 Compact umbrellas at list price $5.00 each
- The buyer is quoted a trade discount of 40% and 15%.
- Terms are 3/10, n/30

Save and print your work.

☼ HINT   You may find the text you enter will not fit properly in the cell. **Wrap** the text as described in Chapter 1.

Practice Problem 7.3

In previous chapters, you have practiced completing a preprogrammed spreadsheet and completing a spreadsheet of your own creation. In this practice problem, you will be asked to complete a case study analysis for three vendors using the partially preprogrammed spreadsheet found in the file labeled **Practice7.3.xls**. The case study below will ask you to use your knowledge of dating, discounts, terms of sale, and pricing to select the most appropriate supplier for a shipment of beaded capri pants necessary to complete Fashion Frenzy's spring assortment.

☀ HINT   You will want to read the case study thoroughly before beginning the assignment and refer back to it often as you work.

CASE STUDY: Jillian Green, the owner/buyer for Fashion Frenzy, visited the Atlanta Apparel Mart looking for a vendor who might have a suitable offering of the stretch, beaded capri pants she needed to complete the spring assortment for her boutique in Wilmington, NC. Fashion Frenzy is a trendy boutique in downtown Wilmington that caters to middle-to-upper-income, fashion-forward women. Jillian spent her first day at the mart meeting and negotiating with three vendors who she determined could offer the product she desired. Exhausted, she has come back to the hotel with the following notes:

---

84 units needed

Miss Sophisticate	Linear	BBX
$22.95/unit	$25/unit	$21.60/unit
FOB Store	FOB Sunnydale Warehouse	FOB Shipping Point
Trans. 1.5%	Trans. 1.5%	Trans. 1.5%
Location: Wilm. NC	2/10 EOM	Location: China
3/10, n/30	Ship: 2/15	2/10, n/30
Ship: 2/15		Ship: 2/15
		Supplies GAP

WE WILL TAKE CASH DISCOUNT!!!
Red, Green, Black, White, Orange*, Turquoise*, sizes 2–14, 2 each color, 2 each size?
*fashion colors/hot trends

Your day, as the assistant buyer, has been spent at the hotel with a laptop inputting orders and vendor notes from the recent trip to Chicago where much of the rest of the assortment was purchased. When Jillian returns to the room, she hands you her notes and asks you to prepare an analysis of each vendor's offering along with your vendor recommendation for the boutique. She explains that she has made dinner arrangements with a key supplier for the boutique. Unfortunately, though she would love to have you along, she must have this analysis and recommendation by the time she returns so that she can make a final decision and fax the order before leaving for the 7:30 A.M. flight you have booked the next morning. "I'll bring you back a burger," she calls back to you as she runs out the door. "Have fun!"

Using the notes Jillian gave you, complete the vendor analysis form and then fill in the recommendation form provided at the bottom of the page. List at least one strength and one weakness for each vendor based on the information given (e.g., location, price, cash discount, transportation).

You may want to refer to the definitions provided at the beginning of this chapter to help you with the formulas. By now, you should be quite comfortable working with Excel spreadsheet formulas.

You can type in strengths and weaknesses much like you would in a word processing program. Just place your cursor in the cell in which you wish to start typing (e.g., **B23**) and do not hit return until you have completed your comment.

Be sure to read the notes carefully and refer back to them often. Remember: The results are only as good as the information and formulas *you* type in! Save and print your work.

 HINT   You can use your text and/or previous lessons if you should need to refresh your memory of formulas or formatting techniques.

INDEX